M000098446

Rock-A-Bye-Bye Baby

Sue Hurst

© Sue Hurst. All rights reserved. No part of this publication may be reproduced, distributed, or transmitted in any form or by any means, including photocopying, recording, or other electronic or mechanical methods, without the prior written permission of the author, except in the case of brief quotations embodied in critical reviews and certain other noncommercial uses permitted by copyright law.

ISBN (Print): 978-1-09837-863-9

ISBN (eBook): 978-1-09837-864-6

To my parents,
Morrie and Rose Shurman,
who loved and adored me and
gave me an amazing life

Contents

PART I:
Longing

Chapter 1:

Turned Upside-Down

"YOU'RE ADOPTED!" my older sister screamed as a final, vicious jab while she was bullying me again. "And your mom didn't want you!"

I froze for a second and then cried out, "What? What are you talking about?"

My nine-year-old brain couldn't grasp my sister's words. "Adopted?" I thought. "My mom didn't want me? But my mom is right here!"

I was simultaneously confused and devastated. My stomach was in knots, and I felt like I was going to pass out. In an instant, my whole world was turned upside-down.

My sister, Cele, was six years older than me. I was used to her torturing and picking on me, but this was different. This was a whole new level of cruelty. I could see that she enjoyed my reaction. She had an evil look in her eyes that I will never forget.

My thoughts were interrupted by my mom telling Cele to go to her room. As Cele slowly sauntered down the hallway toward her bedroom, she turned her head toward me with that look. She knew she had just unlocked Pandora's box.

I ran after her, shouting, "I hate you!" That's the last thing I remember before I stumbled over Cele's outstretched leg, hit my head on the floor, and blacked out.

When I came to, my mom was kneeling next to me, stroking my head. She scooped me up, took me into the dining room, and sat me down, away from my sister. I was still in shock from being knocked out, and still reeling from what Cele had said.

"Mom, what is she talking about?" I asked. "What does 'adopted' mean? Why did she say that my mom didn't want me? Mom, do you still love me? Are you my mom?"

"Sweetheart, of course I love you. Of course, I am your mom."

She could see my tears, and I could see hers.

"Honey, let me explain what 'adopted' means," she continued. "This is complicated. It's something that Daddy and I were planning on telling you when you were a little older.

"Sometimes mommies can't have their own babies. Sometimes mommies need help. I wasn't able to get pregnant, so I needed someone's help.

"I wasn't able to give birth to you or to Cele. I needed someone to help me have babies."

At nine years old, I knew nothing about how a baby came into the world.

I could tell my mom was struggling to find the right words to explain how I came to be part of this family. She continued, "When Daddy and I knew that we wanted to start a family, we had to get help. There are a lot of women who can have babies, but are unable to take care of them, so they need our help, too.

"Daddy and I were lucky that we were able to find a nice, sweet young girl who needed our help. We fell in love with you right away. We knew that you were born just for us.

"You are our daughter, and we are so happy that you came to us."

I was still struggling to try to understand everything that she was saying. I started to ask a slew of questions. "Where is she? Who is she? Is she coming back to get me?"

My mom had the difficult task of trying to give me answers, all while trying to calm me down and wipe away my tears. She was doing her best, but I began to sob and couldn't stop. I was still so confused and hurt.

When my dad came home, he had a sad look on his face, like he knew what had transpired. My mom must have called him at work, so he already knew my little heart had been broken.

My parents took me outside and sat me down. Then they explained as best they could how they had adopted Cele and then me. For a split second, a wave of comfort came over me when I realized that Cele was not my "real" sister. It made so much sense. That's why she was so mean to me!

My parents also explained that they felt they told Cele about her adoption when she was too young. She was very confused and had a hard time understanding. Because they saw how my sister struggled, my parents didn't want to make the same mistake twice. They felt it would be best to wait until I was a little older to tell me the truth.

As we sat in the backyard, the sun started setting. We had talked way past the dinner hour. From the backdoor, Cele yelled something about eating. She was clearly upset that my parents were spending so much time with me.

In an attempt to cheer me up and make me laugh, as my dad always did, he wrapped up the conversation with, "We saw a lot of babies before we saw you. You were the cutest baby of the bunch. We picked you because all of the other babies were ugly!"

With that, we all smiled and tried to have as normal of an evening as we possibly could.

• • •

I thought that maybe since the secret was out, Cele would be more kind and start to treat me a little differently. But, she didn't. Her horrible behavior toward me only escalated. She really felt as if I were my parents' favorite.

Cele, me, and Dad in 1951, when Cele was ten and I was four

Cele was a mischievous girl. To ensure that I wouldn't report her bad behavior to my parents, she would stand over me, bend my thumbs all the way back, and threaten to kill me if I said anything. And

I believed her. At fifteen, Cele was five foot eight and weighed about 170 pounds. I was a skinny little nine-year-old who was constantly walking on eggshells around her.

My parents were wonderful. They adored me and provided for me in every way. I couldn't have asked for better parents. But after that day, I started wondering about this mystery woman—my real mother. Who was she? Was she someone famous? Was she coming back for me someday? At nine years old, I just couldn't understand why she couldn't or wouldn't keep me. I wondered how she could have just given me away, and what I possibly could have done to make her not want me. I began thinking of my real mother every day, wanting more information, wanting to find her.

Chapter 2:

Morrie and Rose

MY PARENTS, MORRIE AND ROSE, were raised in Chicago, Illinois, and were the children of Jewish immigrants—Dad's parents came to America from Russia and Lithuania and Mom's from Russia.

Dad was the oldest of four. He had one younger sister and two younger brothers. His dad owned a Kosher wholesale meat distributing company as well as a hotel, both of which did very well. My grandfather provided a lavish lifestyle for his wife and children. They had a maid, a butler, a driver, and a chef. They also owned a cottage on Lake Muskegon in Michigan, where the whole family vacationed each summer.

Mom was the youngest of five. She had three brothers and one sister. My grandfather owned a barbershop and my grandmother kept house. In 1925, when my mom was eleven, her father died suddenly, leaving his thirty-eight-year-old widow to support the family on her own. My grandmother had never worked outside the home, but she found a job as a cook in a restaurant. She also cleaned houses.

My mom would often tell me how hard life was after her dad died and how her mom struggled to put food on the table. Fortunately, my uncles were soon out of high school and working, so they helped support the family. By 1930, they had also taken in a tenant to make ends meet.

Love at First Sight

In 1934, my dad and his brother George were working in one of the family's Kosher meat markets. One day, a middle-aged woman walked in accompanied by a much younger woman. My dad looked up, caught one glimpse of the young lady with brown hair and blue eyes, and was completely smitten. And as the cliché goes, he leaned over to his brother and said, "That's the girl I'm going to marry!"

Mom, around 1932

My mom was that beautiful young woman, and she was terribly shy. After she visited the meat market a few more times, my dad finally asked her to go on a date with him. However, he neglected to tell her that they were going to his cousin's Bar Mitzvah at the Drake Hotel and that it was a formal affair. My mom had come straight from her job as a social worker, so she was wearing a business suit under her trench coat. All of the other ladies were wearing evening gowns and fur coats. My mom had never seen such opulence. The diamonds were something out of a magazine. She didn't feel that she fit in with this elite social scene and could sense the cold stares and judgment. My dad was very handsome, and my mom sensed that the eligible women were vying for his attention. He was wearing a tuxedo and had a strong resemblance to, and was often mistaken for, Humphrey Bogart.

As the evening progressed, Mom became aware of the social status my father's family held. When she was introduced to his parents and other family members, she was graceful and elegant as always. She charmed her future in-laws, even though she refused to take off her trench coat. My father asked her to dance, and she felt uncomfortable approaching the dance floor. With his calm demeanor, my dad said she was the most beautiful woman in the room. "With a face like this, who's looking at your coat?"

Though it was a somewhat awkward first date, he didn't stop pursuing her, and she didn't push him away.

My parents got engaged in December of 1934. My dad's mom wanted to throw a large, lavish wedding. My dad was her oldest son, after all, and the first son to marry. But my mom didn't have the money for a wedding dress, let alone a fancy wedding. She couldn't ask her own family for money because they were struggling to make ends meet.

One Friday afternoon in February 1935, my parents were discussing the wedding and my mom's discomfort when my dad suddenly said, "Well, let's elope!"

Mom looked at him for a few seconds and then said, "Okay. When?"
"How about right now!" my dad replied.

So, they did! My mom called her best friend and asked if her dad, who was a rabbi, would marry them. My parents raced across town to get to the rabbi's apartment before sundown, since Shabbat was rapidly approaching. My parents called everyone they could, but it was so last minute not many of them could make it. It truly was a small, intimate ceremony.

My mom's family was unable to make it on such short notice. My dad's two brothers, his father, and a few friends attended, but they still didn't have enough men for a minion—a quorum of ten Jewish men required for certain religious obligations. My dad quickly went down to the street to look for someone to complete the minion. He saw a sweet, little old man and asked, "Excuse me sir, could you help me out? I'm trying to get married."

It turned out that the old man was Jewish and knew what a minion was. He agreed and went upstairs with my dad, but he was barely able to walk. My dad was having a panic attack because he didn't think the man would make it up the stairs before the sun went down.

The ceremony was simple and sweet, just like my mom. Her mother-in-law could tell that the girl marrying her son was doing so out of pure love, not because of the money and fanfare. My mom really captured her mother-in-law's heart that day.

Mom was twenty and Dad was twenty-four when they married and moved into a small apartment in downtown Chicago. Their rent was thirty-five dollars a month. They were young and in love and making plans for their future.

Dad and Mom with their books around 1937

Health Issues

Starting a family is something that my parents wanted to do right away. They tried for many years, unsuccessfully, to get pregnant.

Then my parents discovered my mom was suffering from fibroids—noncancerous growths in her uterus that caused heavy bleeding. My dad had to rush her to the hospital one day because she was losing so much blood. She was whisked into an operating room. At one point, the doctor came out to speak with my father.

"We need your permission to perform a hysterectomy," the doctor said. Did the doctor finish his statement with the words "to save her life"? I don't know. But the urgency was there, and my poor dad had to make a life-changing decision without consulting my mom, the person that decision would affect the most.

My dad felt he had no choice. He couldn't take a chance on losing his wife.

When my mom woke up, my dad had to deliver the horrible news that she had a hysterectomy and that she would be unable to have children. My mom was devastated, and the decision put a heavy strain on their marriage. My mother suffered deeply with depression after that surgery. She felt empty and incomplete.

It took a while for my mother to emotionally recover, but a few years later, my parents began the adoption process. In 1941, my parents adopted their first child, Cecilia, nicknamed Cele. She was named after my father's mother.

War Years

By that point, World War II had already begun, and soon after the United States became involved. My grandfather's meat distributing business began to suffer because meat was being rationed as a result of the war. My dad decided it was a good time to leave the family meat business and look for work elsewhere.

At first, he worked as an apprentice to my uncle (my mom's sister's husband), who was a plumber. When plumbing jobs in Chicago became scarce, my dad and uncle traveled to other states—Alabama, South Carolina, Tennessee, Louisiana, Indiana, and West Virginia—in search of work. They were gone for weeks and months at a time, leaving my mom, Cele, my aunt, and my two cousins alone.

My Dad would write and send money when he could. He sent one postcard from Leeville, Louisiana, in November 1942. My mom, Cele, aunt, and cousins were living in Terre Haute, Indiana:

Dear Rose,

Well, baby, we started working this morning—7–10 hours, 162 1/2 hr's not bad. "Shurman the Plumber." I never saw so many soldiers in all my life. They got all the women sewed up here. Work is in the camp hospital. It's Camp Polk (an Army Base). The job is supposed to be till Christmas. I've got my fingers crossed that I can only hang on—kinda miss you, can't you send me a piece of mail? We're living in a 2x4 farmhouse, no light, no toilet, no nothing—looking for a letter.

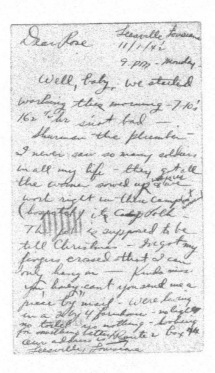

Postcard from Leeville, Louisiana, November 1942

In April 1943, he sent a postcard from Charleston, West Virginia. The women and children were still in Indiana.

Rose and Da Da [he called Cele Da Da for some reason],

Just got thru eating dinner & believe me I really packed it away. Today is a big day in my life. I took possession of a private room and bath. For an hour after work I took a bath, shave, washed hair and cut my nails. Well today is pay day eve, that is the best thing about this job (to me). We bought our foreman a bottle of liquor a piece. It was his birthday. Next to his wife he loves liquor or vice versa. I feel the same way.

Morrie

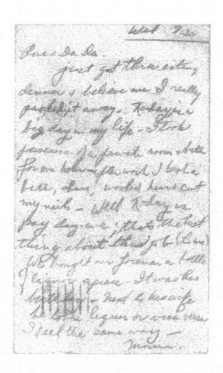

Postcard from Charleston, West Virginia, April 1943

That was my Dad's sense of humor. He never drank, so I find this postcard hysterical!

My dad wrote many more postcards and letters over the next two years, while he and my uncle were traveling around the country. Unfortunately, where they laid their head at night was often like the 2x4 farmhouse with no light and no toilet.

I never knew these postcards and letters existed until after Mom passed away. My daughter, Tracy, and I were cleaning out a storage cabinet. As we were removing some old, rusty cleaning supplies, we came across a small box. At first, we thought it was junk because it was so filthy. We opened it and found my dad's correspondence from those war years. What a hidden treasure!

Fresh Start in California

In the latter part of 1943, the two families headed to California, in search of warmer climate and, hopefully, more job opportunities. They couldn't find housing or steady work in Los Angeles, so the group traveled north and ended up in Pismo Beach, a small oceanfront community on California's Central Coast. My mom, sister, aunt, and cousins stayed in a quaint cottage in Pismo, while my dad and uncle stayed in Los Angeles, traveling to various day jobs. My dad sent money to my mom whenever he got paid. He would include a note saying things like, "I'm sending you some money. We got three days' worth of work today. We've worked here. We've worked there. We're still looking." It was too expensive to drive to Pismo Beach every weekend, so Dad and Uncle Morrie made the drive once every month or two.

Because World War II was still in full swing, some of my dad's jobs supported the war effort. For a while he and my uncle worked at Port Hueneme Naval Base in Ventura County, about an hour north of Los Angeles. My cousin Marcia later told me that she overheard a conversation that led her to believe that our dads worked on the atomic bomb while at the naval base. She remembers it was very hush-hush. My father and uncle never talked about it.

Back in Pismo Beach, my mom and Aunt Mary occupied their time during the day by walking the children to the local library. That's when my mother began to develop her passion for reading and collecting books. Each evening, the women and children had to abide by curfew laws because enemy ships were prowling the coast. They stayed in at night with the lights out and blackout shades drawn. It was a scary and stressful time for two young mothers without their husbands, yet they did their best to stay calm and keep their children at ease.

This arrangement continued for about a year. Finally, in 1944, both families were reunited and settled in Hollywood, California. About two years later, my parents had saved enough money to purchase a home in the Los Angeles area. Shortly after, my father and grandfather opened their own wholesale meat distributing business.

Chapter 3:

My Early Years

LESS THAN A YEAR AFTER THEY MOVED into their new house, my parents added another baby to the family: *me*. Certain details surrounding my adoption are still unclear. What is certain is that I was born in May 1947 in Los Angeles, California, to a young, unwed teenager. I became a member of the Shurman family when I was three days old.

Being Jewish

A couple of years after I was adopted, my mom's mother moved in with us. She's in some of my earliest memories, standing in our kitchen and cooking with my mom. They always had something delicious on the stove: a pot of chicken soup, a pot roast, brisket, potato kugel, baked chicken, and much more.

I also remember my grandmother sewing my clothes on her treadle sewing machine, the same sewing machine I learned to sew on. Unfortunately, I didn't get my grandma's sewing genes. I had a hard time threading the needle, let alone trying to sew something! To this day, I have my grandmother's sewing machine in our home, and I have several framed family photos displayed on the machine's closed cover.

Me in the dress my grandma made for me, July 1950

My grandmother didn't live with us very long. Her health had been declining when she moved in, and she passed away in December 1950 when I was three. I remember my mom telling me how much my grandmother adored me.

The same year my grandmother moved in with us, my parents joined the small Burbank Jewish Community Center. At first, they only attended Friday night services, but after my grandmother's death, they really immersed themselves in the synagogue. Mom became a leader among the women and served as president of the sisterhood for several years. Dad helped with fundraising and bringing in new members. He also served as president of the synagogue for several years.

We attended Friday night Shabbat services as a family. I didn't understand any of the prayers because they were all in Hebrew, but I loved the punch and cookies served afterward. I still remember those fabulous poppyseed cookies! When I was five or six, I started attending Sunday school, which continued throughout my childhood.

As a youngster, I quickly learned that being Jewish made me different. At Christmastime our house was the only one on the block without Christmas lights or a tree. When our elementary school choir put on the annual Christmas pageant, I was the only kid not singing the words "Jesus Christ." Mom told me I couldn't. In fifth grade, when the rest of my classmates received weekly off-campus Christian or Catholic education, known as Religious Release, I was the only one who stayed behind. I spent that hour each week sitting by myself in the library or cafeteria. As far as I know, I was the only Jewish kid in my class, and maybe in the whole school. I felt ostracized, awkward, and alone.

Kids in my class made fun of me because I was different, and so did some kids in my neighborhood. The teasing only increased in sixth grade when I started attending Hebrew School two days a week. We had forty kids on our block, and in elementary school we all played outside in the afternoon. Once I started Hebrew School, however, I had to go in earlier than everyone else. The conversation would go something like this when I said I had to leave:

"Why do you have to go in?"

"I'm going to Hebrew School."

"Oh, that's right. *You're a Jew.*"

I was a shy kid and I didn't stand up for myself. And I never told my parents about the teasing. I just wanted to be like everyone else. It was so hard for me, being different from all the other kids. The only upside was that I had eight days of Hanukkah. And let's be honest—you can't go wrong with a good corned beef sandwich on rye with a few kosher pickles!

Longing

Around 1955 our congregation outgrew our small synagogue, and they found a new location. I remember attending the groundbreaking ceremony with my parents, mainly because actress Debbie Reynolds also attended the festivities.

Debbie Reynolds grew up in Burbank. She attended John Burroughs, the same high school I would later attend. She was crowned Miss Burbank in 1948. Shortly after that, she signed a seven-year contract with Warner Bros. Studios. Debbie Reynolds went on to star in movies such as *Singing in the Rain* (1952) and *The Unsinkable Molly Brown* (1964). Some may remember her as the mother of actress Carrie Fisher.

I always wanted to be like Debbie Reynolds. I thought she was so pretty, and she had red hair just like me. When I was a little older, I even fantasized that she was my birth mother. I thought maybe she had given me up for adoption because she was too busy and couldn't take care of me. I reasoned that if my birth mother was someone important like Debbie Reynolds, then it was okay that she gave me up because she was working on her career, and she would come back for me.

Ironically, many years later, my daughter moved into the house across the street from Debbie Reynolds's former home.

From the day I learned I was adopted, I longed to know more about my birth mother: who she was, why she gave me up, when she was coming back for me. The longing sat in the back of my heart and mind, at times more at the forefront than at others. I didn't share these thoughts with my parents because I didn't want to hurt them. I didn't tell them that even though they provided for me in every way, I still felt incomplete. I always felt like something was missing. I thought if I could just find my birth mother, everything would be okay. I also very much wanted to get away from my nightmare of a sister.

As a child I wondered if I would walk to the mailbox someday and find a letter from my birth mom. Or maybe she would just show up at my house. And I always thought it was going to be Debbie Reynolds. I just knew it! When Debbie had a hotel in Las Vegas, I fantasized about going to see her there. I would go to a show and afterward pop back-stage and say, "Hey, I think you might be my mom." And I had these dreams as an adult! I was disappointed when I found out Debbie prob-ably wasn't old enough to be my mother.

Many years later, I looked up Debbie Reynolds on the Internet and found out her birth name was Mary Frances. *Now that's a good Catholic name!* I thought.

Cele

For years I longed for a nicer sibling. Someone nice and fun to be with. Someone to play games with at night. Someone who would under-stand the anti-Semitism and feeling out of place. Someone completely unlike Cele.

When Cele was about fourteen or fifteen, putting me around eight or nine, my mom drove us to a large office building in Hollywood every few weeks or so. Once inside, my mom and sister were greeted by a woman who ushered them into her office.

My mother never explained why I had to sit, alone, in a waiting room for what seemed like a good hour. It wasn't until years later my mother explained that she had been taking my sister to a psychiatrist. Cele had problems that I'll never understand. She had a hard time in school, mostly with her anger. She was very cruel to me, and my par-ents wanted to diffuse her temperament, but these therapy sessions did nothing to change her attitude.

When I was in elementary school, my parents would leave Cele to babysit me when they went out. I dreaded being left alone with her. Cele was moody and mean, and I never knew what to expect. We didn't sit on the couch and chat and share popcorn on these nights. She would stay in her bedroom or on the phone, while I just sat by myself and watched television.

One time when I was about ten, my parents left for the evening and I settled on the couch to watch *I Love Lucy*. Cele came into the living room with my dad's car keys and said, "Come on. Let's go."

"Where are we going?" I asked.

"Don't worry about it. Just get in the car!" she shouted.

Cele was sixteen at the time, and she wasn't supposed to drive without one of my parents with her. I got in the back seat of the station wagon and shut the door.

We drove in silence for about twenty minutes. Finally, she pulled over on a busy street and parked the car. Before she got out, she said, "Stay here and don't move!"

Suddenly, it dawned on me: she was leaving me there, in the car, alone.

"Where are you going?" I asked, fighting the panic rising in my gut.

"None of your business. Just stay quiet and don't get out of the car." And then she got out, shut the door, and left. I slid down in the seat and tried to hide.

I don't know how long I waited like that, hunched down, fearful someone was going to break in and harm or kidnap me. Was it twenty minutes, or maybe forty-five? I could see people walking by the car, and I just tried to stay out of sight. My thoughts raced. I was petrified.

I finally heard voices and the sound of car keys. Cele wasn't alone. Some guy opened the passenger door while she got in behind the steering wheel. Neither one of them spoke to me, so I just stayed quiet. I sat up and stared out the window.

About twenty minutes later, we pulled up in front of our house. Once we got inside, Cele commanded, "Stay in the living room and watch TV. And be quiet." Then she and the guy disappeared into my sister's bedroom at the back of the house.

Sometime later, the two of them came into the living room and headed toward the front door. Over her shoulder, Cele said, "Let's go." We repeated the twenty-minute drive, dropped the guy off, and came back home.

Once inside, Cele grabbed my hand and pulled my thumb all the way back. She snarled into my face, "If you ever tell mom and dad, I'll kill you." I believed her.

This turned out to be the first of many trips to the United Service Organization, or USO, in Hollywood. Each trip followed the same pattern, the same fearful waiting in the car, the same threat if I tattled. Cele scared the hell out of me, so I couldn't tell her that I didn't want to go. She wouldn't leave me at home because she knew I would run to the neighbor's or to my best friend Linda's house.

Cele came back with a different guy each time. I had no clue what she was doing with the guys in her bedroom. I was only ten years old. I was curious, but I fought the urge to spy on her because I was afraid of what she would do if she caught me.

Finally, after about twenty or so visits to the USO, Cele hooked one. His name was Don. He was a young soldier who had been stationed at Camp Pendleton near San Diego. Unlike the other guys who never said a word to me, Don was nice to me. He ended up in the military because he was given an ultimatum by a judge. He either had to go to jail or join the Marines.

My parents were so disappointed that Cele dropped out of high school at seventeen and married Don. I, on the other hand, wanted to throw a party! Without a doubt, Cele's wedding day was the happiest day of my short life. Finally, no more threats, no more harassment, and no more cruelty. I was free. Hallelujah!

From the time she was a child, Cele struggled—mentally, emotionally, and physically—and things didn't improve after she got married. She had two sons with Don before they divorced. Cele married and divorced several times over the next forty years.

All Vanilla

After Cele married, I had a pretty great life. Actually, except for Cele and the bullying about being Jewish, my whole childhood was fairly idyllic and uneventful. There was never any family drama, and my parents were always even-tempered, loving, and supportive. My childhood was filled with bicycle riding, roller skating, piano lessons, hopscotch, walking to Martino's Bakery, going to the movies, and playing football and baseball in the street with all of the other neighborhood kids.

Among the forty kids on our block, one, Linda, became my lifelong friend and the kind of sister I had always wanted but never had in Cele. Linda and I met when we were about four years old, and we were in the same grade at school. We did everything together. We played hopscotch and dress up, we rode our bicycles together, and we often walked to the corner store for Hostess Twinkies. I spent a lot of time at Linda's house after school, partly because I didn't want to be home with my sister, and partly because her mom made us the best homemade French fries. She would cut up the potatoes, scoop out shortening from the huge can of Crisco, and fry the potatoes in a cast-iron skillet. Those French fries were such a treat. My mom was very health conscious and didn't fry anything!

Linda and I also tested out being "bad girls" together. One time I stole a cigarette from my mom's pack. We snuck out to Linda's backyard playhouse to smoke it, but her younger brother caught us. He threatened to tell Linda's parents, so we bribed him with a quarter to keep quiet. We also used to walk to the neighborhood pharmacy to buy candy bars. One time we wanted to buy a few glamour magazines too, but we only had enough money for one. We took our candy and magazine up to the counter and paid. When the pharmacist turned his back, we grabbed three more magazines, stuffed them behind the one we bought, and left the store. We were terrified of being caught! So much so that we never stole again—the fear cured us. We never went into that pharmacy again either. Any time I went there with my mom to get a prescription filled, I stayed in the car.

When we were in fifth or sixth grade, Linda and I even cut class. Linda forged a note saying we needed to get out of school early. We came back to my house, played dress up in my mom's clothes, and just hung out.

The next day the school called my mom: "Hi, Mrs. Shurman, Did you write a note to get Susie out of school early yesterday?" Well, of course she didn't. I don't remember my punishment for that adventure.

Linda and I were also budding entrepreneurs. My parents and I used to vacation in Pismo Beach each summer. I would walk along the beach and collect oyster shells. When I got home, Linda and I would glue marbles to the bottom of the shells and go door to door selling them as ashtrays. We mostly spent the money on our Twinkie habit. We were the Twinkie Queens, after all! Sometimes with our proceeds, we would walk down to Martino's Bakery for one of their famous glazed teacakes.

Some of my favorite childhood memories involved spending two weeks each summer at my aunt and uncle's house in Los Angeles. My cousin Phyllis was a year and a half older than me, and we were very close. Aunt Mary and Uncle Morrie adored me and treated me like a princess. My aunt knew I loved bacon and that I couldn't have it at home because we never ate pork. She would make me bacon and eggs several times a week. Of course, we never told my mom. It was our little secret.

Me and Linda dressed up for Hayseed Day at school, 1961

During these visits, my aunt and uncle would take Phyllis and me to Palm Springs for the weekend. We would stay in a hotel, go shopping, and eat out—things my family didn't do very often because my dad worked six days a week in the meat market. We also went cherry picking in the fields outside of Palm Springs. Every night we soaked in the glorious hot springs.

Phyllis's sister, Leila, and Leila's husband, Eddie, used to take us water skiing on their boat. We had so much fun on those summer trips. Aunt Mary and Uncle Morrie also hosted various family functions and get-togethers. At Thanksgiving dinner each year, they would invite thirty to forty friends and family members to join. After my uncle died of a heart attack in the 1970s, my aunt sold the house, and my parents' home became the party house. My parents loved to entertain, and through these cookouts and get-togethers, they taught me the importance of family. Both sides of our family were invited to every event. Everyone got along, and we always had fun spending time together.

Chapter 4:

Junior High/High School

JUNIOR HIGH BROUGHT CHANGES, both good and bad. We no longer had Religious Release, which eased my sense of being different on campus. However, I also started attending Hebrew School much more often in preparation for my Bat Mitzvah. This meant I had very little time to spend with my best friend, Linda.

Around the same time, a new girl named Kathy moved in a few doors down from Linda, and Linda started hanging out with her a lot. Linda even switched schools so that she could attend the same junior high school as Kathy. I felt very alone. Of course, now I realize Linda needed someone to hang out with because I wasn't around much, but at the time it was hard for me to accept that she had found another friend. I so wished I didn't have to go to Hebrew School. I wanted to be with my best friend.

I continued walking to school with another girl named Michelle. Not long after that, however, Michelle's parents divorced, and Michelle had to move an hour away to live with her dad. I had never known anybody whose parents got divorced, and I didn't understand why Michelle had to go live with her father.

After I lost Michelle, my sense of isolation increased. Here I had a house free of Cele and a great bedroom in the rear of the house, but I had no one to share it with. Eventually Kathy moved, and Linda started attending my junior high school again. I had my best friend back! I was elated.

Bat Mitzvah

The apex in a young Jewish girl's education is the Bat Mitzvah—a coming-of-age ceremony that takes place on her thirteenth birthday. Though I wasn't thrilled about being Jewish, I knew I had to complete this important milestone. It's what all those years of Hebrew School had been leading up to.

My dad and mom had told me that my birth mother was not Jewish. In the Jewish religion, if your mother is not Jewish, you are not considered a Jew, so I had to go through a conversion ceremony before my Bat Mitzvah.

My conversion took place at the University of Judaism in Los Angeles. It was a short ceremony in which I had to chant several prayers in Hebrew. The rabbi then said a blessing over me and submerged me into a body of water three times. The submersion part of the ceremony is called a mikvah.

The day before my Bat Mitzvah, I was incredibly nervous. It didn't matter that I had spent the last few years studying, memorizing, and practicing the haftarah section I would be chanting. Giving a speech at school or being called on by the teacher gave me a stomachache, and now I had to stand in front of the entire congregation and chant in Hebrew for approximately thirty minutes. I got myself so worked up that I started feeling nauseous that day in class. I went to the nurse's office, and someone called my mom to come and take me home. She picked me up, and just before I got in the car, I vomited in the street.

On the day of my Bat Mitzvah, I sat with my parents during the regular service, stomach churning and hands sweating, but I put on my best "I got this" face for Mom and Dad. Then the rabbi called my name, and I slowly made my way to the bema. I turned toward the sea of a couple hundred people, including all of my aunts, uncles, and cousins, plus the whole congregation—this was a big deal; I was Morrie and Rose Shurman's daughter, after all!—but I never made eye contact with anyone. I stared at the haftarah and started chanting. I knew if I tried to look up, I would lose my train of thought, so I just chanted, head down with my eyes focused on the words in front of me. Somehow, I did it, without a single mistake. Then I walked off the bema, sat down, and breathed a huge sigh of relief. It was over!

Afterward, we had a lavish, catered celebration. It was wonderful, and let's be honest—I loved all of the gifts! That was the best part.

Dad, me, and Mom on my Bat Mitzvah day, 1960

After my Bat Mitzvah I began confirmation classes. Confirmation marks the last year of formal Jewish education for a young person. I also joined the B'nai B'rith Girls group at the synagogue, a youth group for young ladies; the boys' group was called Aleph Zadik Aleph. We went on field trips to Big Bear or the beach, had dances, and attended get-togethers at different members' homes, including ours. The youth group helped me develop more self-confidence, and gave me a great group of Jewish friends. With them I wasn't the only Jewish kid.

Mom and Dad

Mom was very dedicated to our synagogue and served there alongside my dad in many capacities. She was also active in the community. For her service over the years, Mom received numerous merits, awards, and recognitions—including a scholarship to the University of Judaism as a reward for being president of the sisterhood.

My mom studied religious education at the University of Judaism, where the classes were taught in Hebrew. Mom loved it! She graduated with a bachelor's degree in Jewish education and then taught Hebrew School at our synagogue.

In 1973, Mom became the librarian at Stephen Wise Temple in Los Angeles. Six years later she became a librarian technician at the University of Judaism and stayed in that position for nearly twenty years.

Mom was in heaven working at the university. She loved books and bought every volume on Judaism she could find. She worked into her early eighties and would have kept on working had it not been for a fall in her driveway in which she broke her wrist in several places. Not being able to type well after that, she regretfully retired.

When my mom first went back to school and attended night classes, my dad would take me out to dinner. We usually went to a local deli or a restaurant that served amazing fried chicken. Sometimes I even got a vanilla ice cream cone with sprinkles. My mom had also started teaching Sunday school by then, so she would leave early on Sunday mornings to go prepare for class and my dad would take me to breakfast. We went to a local place called Albin's Drug Store, and we ate in the coffee shop. I always had the same thing: eggs over medium, hash browns, and white toast. After breakfast, my dad would drop me off at Sunday school, and he would go into the synagogue for meetings with some of the board members. I loved that time alone with my dad. He made me feel so special, like his precious little girl.

Unfortunately, those meals out with my dad ended a few years later when my parents became kosher. No more corned beef. No more fried chicken. No more anything that wasn't kosher. My dad and I were limited to breakfast on Sunday mornings. I really missed having that extra time with him.

In 1960 my dad and his friend, Andy Hart, opened a meat market and named it Shurman-Hart Meats. They owned that business until 1982.

My dad loved his work at the meat market. He enjoyed helping customers and spent time getting to know them over the years. In general, my dad was a jovial guy, always in a good mood, always finding the positive in a situation, always ready to tell a joke and keep the mood light. At work, however, he could be stern. My dad's partner was the easy-going one at the meat market. Dad was no-nonsense, making sure we worked first and had fun second.

When we were fourteen, Linda and I started working on Saturdays at my dad's market. We worked in the back room, wrapping meat. The market provided an incredible learning experience. Over the years I learned every aspect of the business. After starting out wrapping sides of beef, I moved on to counter girl, cashier, delivery girl, and finally my dad's bookkeeper.

Dad and Andy were honest, hardworking men. From them I learned a strong work ethic and how to treat everyone with respect, no matter their race, religion, or background. I worked for my dad for twenty years. It was the best job I ever had.

Me and Linda in our smocks at Shurman-Hart Meats, 1963

High School

Friday nights in high school meant football and basketball games, followed by Bob's Big Boy for hamburgers and fries at the car hop. That is, when my mom would let me go. She was very religious; I think she was more kosher than some of the rabbis! She wanted me to be active in the synagogue, which meant attending Friday night services. But for me, having fun with my friends was more important. My parents recognized this and became more lenient with me as I got older.

In early 1963, my parents put a swimming pool in our backyard. It was finished just in time for my sweet sixteen party. We had hot dogs and hamburgers and my mom made a yummy banana ice cream cake. Everybody raved about that cake. My friends and I had the best time in our new pool, which was the greatest gift of all. After the pool went in, our house became a regular hangout for friends and family.

Me and Linda, 1963

Because we didn't learn our lesson in our last year of elementary school, Linda and I cut class again in high school. This time we went to the beach. We didn't have our driver's licenses yet, so we had to take a couple of buses to get there, and it seemed like it took forever. Because of my fair skin, I came back sunburned.

That night my parents asked, "So, how was school today?"

"It was good," I replied with a sinking feeling in my gut.

"Really? The school called. You wrote another note."

"No, I didn't! Linda wrote it."

"Well, you have been suspended for one day. You're coming to work with me tomorrow, and you're not getting paid," said my dad.

"Okay," I replied. I didn't really view this as punishment because I knew I was going to get a slice of pizza for lunch from the pizza place that was in the same building as my Dad's meat market.

My parents were the best, but they were strict. I had an 11:00 p.m. curfew while the rest of my friends could stay out later, so I started sneaking out at night. My bedroom was in the back of the house, with a door leading outside between my room and the kitchen. I'd sneak out the door, climb over the wall, and run down the street to meet my friends.

The main reason I snuck out was to meet Russell, the boyfriend my parents didn't know I had. He worked at Pizza Pete, in the same building as my dad's meat market. Dad knew who Russell was and wasn't impressed. In fact, after watching Russell flirt with me one day, my father said, "Stay away from that guy."

To Dad, Russell was just a goof-off with a Beatles haircut. He would never be the Jewish attorney or doctor my parents had envisioned for me. But Russell paid attention to me. He was a year older, and he told me I was beautiful—something no boy had ever said. I had never had a boyfriend and never had a boy flirt with me. Russell's attention boosted my ego, and I fell under his spell. I knew my parents wouldn't have approved, so I just didn't tell them.

Russell and I started dating in my senior year. When it came time for prom, I wanted to go with Russell, but I couldn't tell my parents I had been dating him. As far as my parents knew, I had never been on a date with anyone. My parents had once tried to set me up with a nice young man from the synagogue, but I got so nervous I made myself sick and begged my mom to cancel the date a few hours before I was supposed to go out.

Since I knew my parents wouldn't approve of my going with Russell, Linda pretended Russell was her date, and I pretended to go with Linda's date, John. My mom had met John several times when he came to the house with some of our friends to go swimming. My mom thought John was a nice young man, and she was excited that I was going to the prom. My mom took me shopping and bought me a beautiful pale blue dress.

The night of the prom, John came to the door to pick me up while Linda and Russell waited in the car down the street. We quickly switched dates and my parents never found out. John also had to pick me up for our Grad Night at Disneyland. Once again, Linda and Russell waited in the car down the street.

Me and Linda in our prom dresses, June 1965

Plan B

I graduated from high school in 1965 and spent that summer working at my dad's meat market—and secretly dating Russell. Sometimes he would sneak over the wall, and we'd spend time together in my bedroom for a couple hours and then he would sneak back out. One night, however, we both fell asleep and didn't wake up until the next morning.

I got up at 7:00 a.m. as usual, got ready for work, and left by 8:30. Russell was supposed to get up and sneak out right after I left, but he didn't. He fell back asleep. My mom walked into the laundry room, which is right next to my room, and found him sleeping in my bed.

Shortly after that I got a call at work.

"Oh, hi, Mom," I said when I answered.

"You need to come home right now!" my mother yelled. I had never heard her so angry.

My stomach dropped. "Why?"

"I think you know why."

I got into my dad's car and drove home, panic-stricken. I just knew she was currently interrogating Russell. I had no idea how he would answer her questions. I didn't know what I was going to say to my mom when she started questioning me.

When I walked into the house, my mom sent Russell outside and proceeded to ask me the same series of questions she had just asked Russell. She wanted to know who he was, how I knew him, and how long had this been going on. She wanted to know why was he in my bed. I lied and told her Russell had just stopped by. We were talking and he fell asleep. She didn't buy it. I think the fact that he was naked when she found him was a dead giveaway.

"You can't tell Dad!" I pleaded. "I'll leave with Russell if you do."

She sighed and said, "No, no, I won't tell Dad, but you can never see him again."

"Okay," I replied, knowing full well that I wouldn't follow through with that.

A few months later, I was sitting at the dining room table with my mom. Suddenly, I felt sick to my stomach and vomited all over the place. I thought I had the flu.

"You don't have the flu," my mom shouted. "*You're pregnant!*"

"I can't be pregnant!" I protested.

My mom walked into the other room, and I left the house. Linda no longer lived down the street. She lived about six blocks away, but I figured I would just walk there. My mom didn't know where Linda had moved.

As I was walking down the street, my mom pulled up beside me in her car. She rolled down the window and asked, "Where are you going?"

"My friend's house," I said as I kept walking.

My mom told me to get in the car. I told her I didn't want to go home.

"Get in the car, or I will tell your dad," she said." With that, I knew I had no choice. I stopped walking, looked at my mom, and finally got in the car.

A few days later, my mom took me to an obstetrician, who confirmed that I was indeed pregnant. I was in shock. I kept thinking, *This can't happen!* followed by *Oh my God. My dad is going to kill me!*

True to her word, Mom didn't tell Dad. Now, I was going to have to.

Having that conversation with my father was the hardest thing I ever had to do. I was so scared to admit that I had been dating Russell behind his back. When I finally told him the truth, my dad was so disappointed in me. He didn't say a lot in response.

After I told my dad, my parents called Russell and asked him to come to the house. I was scared out of my mind. I had no idea how my father was going to react when Russell walked through the door.

My father was always a gentleman. Anytime he greeted another man, he always shook his hand, but my dad didn't extend his hand to Russell. My mother, always the gracious hostess, didn't even offer him a glass of water.

At one point during the awkward conversation, I remember my dad saying, "Well, I guess you two are going to have to get married." They talked a little longer, and then my dad told Russell it was time for him to leave. I don't remember saying one word during the entire conversation. When Russell left, I didn't even walk him outside.

My parents were so upset and disappointed. They had a hard time believing I had secretly been dating Russell for some time. They really disliked him. My dad saw Russell day to day, flirting with every girl who bought a slice of pizza. And my mom's first meeting with him was when she discovered him naked in my bed, not exactly a great first impression. My parents wanted something better for me, especially after what they went through with Cele. They had seen her get married at seventeen and struggle in a bad marriage with two kids they could barely support. I had just started classes at Los Angeles Valley College, and here I was eighteen and pregnant!

My parents were so desperate for me to avoid my sister's fate. My mom even suggested I get an abortion. I couldn't believe it. I got so mad that I blurted out, "You're not my mom! You can't tell me what to do!" My dad was an even-keeled, mild-mannered guy. He never swore or used bad language. But when I said that to my mom, he was furious.

"You better go outside right now," he said, barely controlling his anger. "You sit out there until you can calm down and come back in here and apologize to your mother."

So, I went out to the backyard and sat on the diving board for a long time. I tried to wrap my head around what the hell I had gotten myself into. I didn't really know Russell. In the year that we had dated, we didn't do anything but sneak around. I hadn't met any of his family, and he hadn't met mine, until now. I had never been to his apartment. I didn't really know any of his friends. I wasn't sure that I was doing the right thing by getting married, but I knew that I wanted to keep my baby. That was the only thing I did know. And the only acceptable way to do that in 1965 was to get married.

I walked back into the house and apologized to my mom and then told my dad that I would marry Russell.

I hated to see the great pain I had caused my parents. I was always the "good girl." I was also scared. My whole life was about to change. I had no idea what I was getting myself into and with whom.

A few months later, on November 3, 1965, Russell and I got married. We had a small civil ceremony at the Los Angeles Courthouse attended by my Aunt Mary; my best friend, Linda; my close friend, Susie; and my parents. Not one of Russell's family members or friends came. I don't know if he even invited them.

After the ceremony, there was no reception, no celebration. Nothing.

We went back to my parents' house so that I could get my clothes and some of my belongings. We drove straight to Russell's apartment in Glendale. And that was it. We didn't go on a honeymoon. We just went off into this unknown world of marriage.

I broke my parents' hearts, though I didn't realize how badly at the time. I was a know-it-all teenager who just wanted to stay out late like her friends and ended up pregnant and married. I dropped out of college and went to work full time at my dad's meat market, while Russell continued working at the pizza place. We made enough to pay rent every month and buy things we needed for the baby. It definitely wasn't what I had dreamed of for myself.

PART II:

Searching

Chapter 5:

The Search Begins

WHILE I WAS PREGNANT, I began wondering again about my "real" mother. I had so many questions. Why did my birth mother give me up? How old was she when she got pregnant? Was she dating my father? Did my birth father know about me? I very much wanted to find her, and I hoped I might get some answers if I started searching.

I knew I needed to go to the courthouse and I knew I needed to be eighteen to make my request, but that was all I knew about the process. During the summer after I graduated from high school, I drove to the Los Angeles Superior Court with a friend.

Once we got to the courthouse, we didn't know where to start. We walked up to one window, and I told the person I wanted to talk to somebody about adoptions. The clerk asked what I wanted to know.

"I'm trying to find my birth mother," I replied.

"Okay. I'll see if I can help you. What's your name? And where and when were you adopted?"

I gave her the information and waited while she stepped away from the window. She returned a few minutes later.

"I'm sorry, but your records are sealed," the clerk said.

"But I'm eighteen now. Do you want to see my driver's license?"

"No, that's not necessary. Your records are sealed."

"What does that mean? How do we go about unsealing them? Do I have to go to court?" I asked.

"If your birth mother doesn't ask to have the records unsealed, you can't get any information about her," she said.

I stood there, extremely disappointed. I had waited all these years, and now this person was telling me that I couldn't get any information.

"So, there's nothing I can do?" I asked.

"No. She has to unseal the records," the clerk replied. "If your birth mother is looking for you, the court will notify you."

I was devastated. I had always hoped that once I turned eighteen and went to the courthouse, I would be able to find my birth mother. Now I realized I might never find her. I didn't even have a name. I had a baby bracelet with the words "M Francis" on it, but what did that mean? Was my birth mother going to name me Mary? Was my birth mother's name Mary? I had no idea.

"I can't believe this," I told my friend.

"Let's go to lunch," my friend suggested, shaking me from my thoughts.

After that first attempt, I was so discouraged. I thought about my birth mother a lot. I wondered if she thought about me, or if she had a family of her own and didn't want me to find her. As much as I wanted to find my birth mother, I also didn't want to hurt my parents. I never told them I went to the courthouse that day, and I didn't make another active attempt to locate my birth mother for many years.

Tracy and Jason

I gave birth to Tracy in June 1966, and even though my parents weren't happy about me getting married so young, they immediately fell in love with my daughter. My mom was working full time so she couldn't watch Tracy after I went back to work. Russell's mom, who lived down the street from our apartment, helped with babysitting. Russell's younger brothers, who were fifteen and seventeen at the time, also helped out on the weekends.

I was a nervous nineteen-year-old mom. I was trying my best to take care of my new daughter, but I had never even babysat a baby and I had never changed a diaper. I was completely unprepared. I just wanted to go back to work, which I did two weeks after I gave birth. With a little help from my mother-in-law, I figured things out and soon adjusted to motherhood.

Having Tracy caused me to think about my birth mother once again. I was so in love with my daughter. I wondered how my birth mother could have just given me away. Was it hard for her? Was she forced to give me away? Did her parents make her do it? I wondered if my mother ever had the chance to hold me or even see me. Or did they just whisk me away? Did my birth mother put the bracelet on my wrist or did the nurse?

Three years after Tracy was born, I gave birth to my son, Jason. This time I took six months off to be with my newborn and three-year-old. As I marveled at my second, beautiful child, I again wondered about my birth mother.

Jason, me, and Tracy, 1970

Tracy and Jason, 1972

Married Life

From the very beginning, I knew that this marriage was a big mistake. We didn't have much money, and I had to figure out how to manage our finances and balance a checkbook, which I had never done. I was too humiliated to go back to my parents to hear the words, "I told you so," and so I buried my unhappiness. I worked days, and Russell worked nights. Very often, he would not return home until two or three in the morning. I felt trapped and very unhappy.

I also felt so alone. All of my friends were attending college or still living at home. They didn't have time for me, and most of my friends didn't like Russell.

I kept hoping that things would improve. From time to time, I thought about my birth mother, but I didn't search for her. Raising two kids, working, and dealing with a troubled marriage occupied most of my time and energy.

Knowing that I broke my parents' heart made me stay in a bad marriage for so many years. My parents never approved of Russell, even though he got a better job as a private investigator and converted to Judaism. In 1970 we even got remarried in the synagogue, but that didn't change my parents' opinion of him.

Migraines

One Saturday night in 1982, I dropped Tracy and her friends off at a school function and had a couple hours before I needed to pick them up, so I went over to my parents' house for a visit. The three of us were sitting at their dining room table when all of a sudden, I was hit with an intense headache. I looked up at the wall clock across the room and realized I couldn't read it. The numbers and hands were all blurry. I freaked out, but didn't say anything about it to my parents. I just said, "Mom, I think I'm going to lay down." When I spoke, my speech sounded slightly slurred, but thank God my parents didn't notice. I panicked and thought, *Oh my God. Did I just have a stroke?*

I slept for an hour or so, and when I woke up, my vision and speech were back to normal, but I was really tired and I still had a headache. I said good-bye to my parents, picked up the kids, and went home.

As I was pulling up in front of my house, I was again overcome with a headache and my vision became blurry. I was so weak that I barely made it up the stairs. I then collapsed into bed, more exhausted than I had ever been in my life.

I was completely incapacitated for the next four days. I could barely get my head up off the pillow because I was so nauseous. I called my boss and told her I had the flu, but I didn't say anything about my blurry vision or slurred speech. I was so scared. I finally contacted my doctor, and he told me to go straight to the hospital.

When my doctor arrived, he performed an angiogram and other tests to rule out a stroke. He also asked about my family history. I told him that I was adopted and had no family medical history. Ultimately, the doctor decided the episode with my vision and speech was the side effect of a powerful migraine.

During this time, Russell and I weren't getting along, so I did everything I could to avoid being home in that unhappy environment. I worked full time Monday through Friday, and on weekends I helped a friend make and sell homemade picnic baskets at trade shows. I was overworking myself and I wasn't getting enough sleep, and my migraines continued.

One night after making picnic baskets, I was driving home when suddenly my leg went completely numb. It just stopped working. When I pulled up to my house, I could barely press the brake pedal down enough to stop the car. My head was pounding and I lost peripheral vision. Somehow, I made it inside and stumbled into bed, where I stayed for the next few days. When I called the doctor, he reminded me

that these kinds of migraines come on if you're under stress or pushing
yourself too hard, which I was, or if you're not getting enough sleep, and
I was not sleeping well at all.

At that point I still hadn't told my parents I had visited the courthouse when I was eighteen. They still held my adoption papers in a safe
deposit box. I had never asked for the papers, and my parents had never
offered to give them to me.

After my parents became aware of my migraines and how often I
was having them, my dad brought it up.

"Something's not right, Susie. You need to know your medical
history, for you and your kids. You should try to find your birth mother.
I have the adoption paperwork from the attorney."

"Yeah, but the records are sealed, Dad," I replied. I then told my
parents about going to the courthouse fifteen years earlier.

"Well, let me call Alan and Bernie," my dad said. Both Alan and
Bernie were judges and friends of my dad who would have done anything within their power to help him.

Dad called, but they gave him the same information I had already
received: the records had been sealed, and there wasn't anything they
could do to unseal them.

A few days later, my dad tried to contact the attorney who had
handled my adoption. When he called the law firm, he was told the
attorney had passed away a few years earlier. They said the firm no longer had my adoption records, and they were unable to give us any additional information.

My dad's friends suggested that I start contacting adoption agencies to get some answers. They specifically mentioned the Alma Society,
a nonprofit organization that helps people connect with birth relatives.
I decided to join and wrote a letter with the little information I had:
where and when I was adopted, the name my parents gave me, and
the name on my baby bracelet. I received a letter back from the Alma

Society saying that my birth mother had not joined, so that was a dead end. I tried a couple other agencies, but again found nothing.

Ever since I found out I was adopted, I wondered about my birth mother. And with the wondering there was a concern of being rejected. I worried that she didn't want to be found. That fear came up again as I joined the Alma Society and other agencies. I was afraid that if I did find her, she wouldn't want to know anything about me. I worried that she had her own family and never told them about me and didn't want them to know about her past.

After getting nowhere with Dad's friends and the agencies, I put the search out of my mind for a while. I was busy with raising kids, working, and everyday life. Plus, I wasn't sure if I wanted to find her and then get my heart broken. But the longing and wondering were always there, lingering in the back of my mind.

Changes

In May of 1986, my daughter, Tracy, moved into her own apartment. After helping her unload the last few boxes, I met my friend Sherry for dinner. She knew I had been unhappy in my marriage. As we ate, Sherry asked, "Why are you still with Russell?"

"Good question," I replied.

I had always believed that it was better for our children to have both parents in the house. Because of this 1950s thinking, I didn't think divorce was an option. In addition, I didn't want to admit to my parents that I was unhappy and had been for the last twenty years.

Sherry had a two-bedroom house. She said that I could stay with her for a couple of days until I figured things out. However, Jason was still in high school and I didn't want to upset the family unit. I struggled with what to do. Finally, I convinced myself that it would be okay to move out since Jason was a young man now and the two men would be fine together.

The next day I took a few days' worth of clothes and went to Sherry's house.

Unfortunately, I had been wrong about leaving Jason with Russell, who didn't deal well with the fact that I had left. He filled Jason's head with things that were not true about me. As hard as this was, however, I knew I couldn't go back.

I stayed with Sherry for a few weeks, and then I got my own apartment. Six months later, Sherry bought a condo in Pasadena and asked me to move in with her, and I did. Russell kept thinking I was coming home, but I was done.

By January 1987, Russell and I were divorced. Still, he kept hoping we would get back together, so one night he called to invite me and some friends to join him at the Magic Castle, a place where magicians perform in Hollywood. He told me that Bob Hurst would be joining him. Bob had trained Russell as a private investigator twenty years earlier, and I had always liked him. He was a friendly, good-looking guy. He occasionally came by the meat market and took me out for a cup of tea.

I was still on the phone with Russell when he suddenly said, "Hold on, my other phone is ringing. Here, talk to Bob while I answer this."

When Bob got on the phone, I said, "You know, you owe me a cup of tea."

"Do you want me to invite Russell along?" Bob asked.

"Hell no!" I replied and laughed.

I did end up going to the Magic Castle with a few of my girlfriends, and we had a great time. It was nice to see Bob again, too.

The next day Bob called and asked me to have lunch with him, and I gladly accepted. When he rang the doorbell to pick me up, one of my favorite Elvis Presley songs was on the radio: "I Can't Help Falling in Love with You." Well, if that wasn't a sign of things to come!

When Bob picked me up in his Corvette, I felt like a schoolgirl. I was so nervous. As soon as we got into the car and started talking, however, I calmed down. He was so easy to talk to. Plus, he opened doors for me and pulled out my chair at the restaurant and acted like such a gentleman. That first date was pure magic.

The next day, Bob asked me to dinner again, and from that point on, we never went a day without seeing each other.

Within three months, I moved in with Bob, and the rest is history. Thirty-two years later, he is still the man of my dreams.

Chapter 6:

Milestones

IN THE EARLY 1990s when I was reaching out to adoption agencies, I decided to call my friend, Ron, who was a Los Angeles County sheriff. Ron searched every database available at that time, to no avail. After coming up empty-handed, he suggested I contact the Department of Social Services (DSS).

My First Glimpse of My Birth Parents

I put it off for a while, but at the beginning of 1993, I finally decided to write the DSS. Eight weeks later I received a response.

I couldn't wait to open the envelope to see what information was inside. This is what I received:

March 29, 1993

Dear Mrs. Hurst:

Enclosed is all the information obtained at the time of your adoption that we can disclose from our file; the Department of Social Services (DSS) does not maintain contact with the parties to an adoption after it has been completed.

The Department or a licensed adoption agency may arrange for contact between an adult adoptee and a birth parent if each has signed a consent for contact. If siblings separated by adoptions are over 21 and each sends in waivers of confidentiality, names and addresses of each may be exchanged. DSS will provide waiver and consent forms only upon request as soliciting consents or waivers is prohibited. We have received your consent form and placed it in your adoption file. To date, we have not received a consent form from either of your birth parents and there have been no inquiries regarding your adoption.

DSS or an adoption agency can receive, maintain, and release designated nonidentifying letters, photos, or other materials to adult adoptees, birth parents, and adoptive parents of minor adoptees upon request.

You may request a copy of your amended birth certificate from the Office of State Registrar, 304 "S" Street, Sacramento, CA 95814. Please contact the State Registrar at (916) 445-2684 for any questions concerning birth certificates or fees.

You may be able to obtain the original birth certificate by petitioning, under Health and Safety Code Section 10439, the superior court in your county of residence or the county of adoption for a court order to have it unsealed. Please contact the county clerk for information on petitioning the court.

Person Requesting Background Information: Adoptee
Name: Susan P. Hurst
Birth Date: May **, 1947

BIRTH MOTHER (Source: Birth Mother)
Descent—Race: Caucasian (descent not reported)
Place of Birth: New York
Age at Birth of Child: 16
Religion: Methodist
Education: She completed the tenth grade.
Occupation: Student

Physical Description: She was 5 feet 3 inches tall, weighed 113 pounds, and had blue eyes, light-brown hair, and a fair complexion.

Special Interests: She enjoyed singing, and she was musically inclined.

Were the Birth Parents Married to Each Other? No

Extended Family:

Parents of Birth Mother: Her mother was 43 years of age and was a housewife. She did not complete high school. Her father was 47 years of age and was employed as a manager for a feed store. He completed high school. They were both in good health.

Siblings: She had two brothers and two sisters.

Marriages: None

Siblings of Adoptee: None

Health: She was in good health. There was no history of functional disorders, hereditary diseases, or abnormalities.

Mother's Health at Birth of Child: The attending physician reported that your mother's general health and physical condition were excellent. There were no complications of pregnancy or delivery. She had a serological test which was negative.

Child's Health at Birth: The attending physician reported that you were in good health at the time of delivery. You were born at 6:32 a.m.

Circumstances of Placement: Your mother decided to place you for adoption because she was unable to care for you adequately. She felt that adoption was the best plan for you. Your birth father did not know of the pregnancy or your birth. Your adoptive placement was arranged by your birth mother's mother.

BIRTH FATHER (Source: Birth Mother)
Your birth father was born in New York of the Caucasian race. He was 20 years of age at the time of your birth. He was 5 feet 8 inches tall with a medium build, and he had black

hair and a fair complexion. He completed high school and was serving in the U.S. Marines. Both of his parents were living. His father was employed by the government. He had one brother and three sisters. He was athletic and he was in good health. Your mother knew of no unfavorable health history in his family background. He was not married. This is all of the information that your birth mother provided about your birth father.

The county clerk in the county where the adoption was granted maintains a closed adoption record. Under Civil Code Section 229.10, it can be opened only by an order of the superior court. Please contact the county clerk for information on petitioning the court for access to documents (relinquishment or consent, agreement, order, report to the court, etc.) filed in the office of the county clerk.

I hope some of the enclosed information answers some of your questions concerning the background of your biological parents. In those instances where unanswered questions remain, please note that the information probably is not in the case record, or else it is considered confidential on the basis that it could be used to reveal the identity or whereabouts of another individual.

Sincerely,
Adoptions Systems Unit

When I finished reading, I was struggling with a range of emotions. Before this, I knew my mother was a very young girl, but that was it. And I hadn't even thought about my birth father. I never imagined that I would find him or know anything about him. I had romanticized that perhaps my birth parents met at Fleet Week in New York City and then went their separate ways.

Now I had all these details about my birth parents, who *did in fact know each other!* My birth mother was able to provide some specific information about my birth father, so they must have had a relationship of some kind. I was overwhelmed and happy and surprised all at once. In all of these years of searching for my mother, I had been focused on learning the circumstance of my adoption and why she gave me away. It never occurred to me that I would ever know anything about my real father.

Although this was much more information than I had before I wrote to the DSS, I felt a little disappointed. I still didn't have names or real leads that could help me find my birth parents. How would I go about finding a twenty-year-old US Marine in 1947? That description fit so many young men.

The letter stated that I could request a copy of my amended birth certificate, so I did. I was hopeful that the certificate would have both of my birth parents' names. I waited about six to eight weeks, but when I finally heard back, the notice said my birth certificate was part of the sealed records.

I told my parents that I had written to the DSS, and I shared the responses I received. My parents felt bad that I was unable to obtain more information and wondered why the DSS couldn't tell me more.

"Well, she's not looking for me," I said. "Unless she asks to have my adoption records unsealed, there's nothing else I can do." It was hard to admit my birth mother wasn't looking for me. She wasn't interested. She probably had her own family, so why did she need me? It was heartbreaking. At this point I was forty-six years old, and I had been searching for most of my adult life. I wondered if she had ever thought to look for me.

After the dead end with Social Services in March 1993, I gave up for a while. I felt stuck, like there was nothing more I could do if my birth mother wasn't searching for me. Every now and then I would receive letters from the Alma Society, but they were the generic type informing me that no one was searching for me. I kept paying my annual dues just in case, but that was the extent of my search for the next eight years. At the back of my mind, I kept thinking about her and worried that I wouldn't find her before she died. At different points over the next several years I would think *I need to find her because now she's sixty … now she's seventy.* In some ways I felt like I was racing against the clock.

Dad

In 1990, when my father was eighty years old, he was diagnosed with prostate cancer. At one point the doctors recommended chemotherapy and radiation, but Dad declined, saying he was too old. He opted for testicular surgery.

Since my parents were getting up in age, Bob and I decided it might be a good time to move closer to their home. We felt that they really needed us. We found a house just down the street from my childhood home where my parents were still living.

About two weeks after we moved in, my father received a Lifetime Achievement Award for his work with the Federation of Jewish Men's Clubs. This was the last in a long line of awards he had received over the years for his work in the Jewish community. In 1956, his name was inscribed in the center of the new synagogue building he had raised money for through tireless fundraising. In 1970, the Federation of Jewish Men's Clubs awarded my dad the prestigious Red Yarmulka Award, and in 1987, the federation gave him the Ma'asim Tovim—the highest recognition one of its members can receive. He was also recognized by the

University of Judaism for his leadership in the university program to advance the cause of Jewish life and learning on the West Coast.

In addition to his work in the Jewish community, my dad was active in the city of Burbank. In 1997, he received two awards for his community service: the Certificate of Special Congressional Recognition award and the Burbank Outstanding American Citizen award.

In February 2001, we were planning a big celebration for my parents' sixty-sixth wedding anniversary and my dad's ninety-first birthday. Then my dad started having some complications with his prostate again. He went into the hospital on Thursday and the celebration was the next evening. We talked about canceling the party, but my dad refused to call it off. He was very active in local politics and had invited nominees he was backing for city council, and he wanted his friends to meet them.

On the way to the party, Tracy stopped at the hospital to visit. She knew that my dad would love a delivery of his favorite candy, a Nestle Crunch bar. She also picked up a pack of playing cards in the hospital gift shop.

She walked into the room and surprised my dad. They played three rounds of gin rummy, and he beat her all three rounds, of course. However, Tracy noticed that he didn't eat the candy bar. That might not sound like a big deal, but Tracy knew something wasn't right.

Moments after Dad's final gin rummy victory, the doctor walked into the room and announced that they were ready to take him in for his blood transfusion. Tracy was taken aback. We had no idea that he was scheduled for a transfusion. He didn't share this with us as he didn't want us to worry. Tracy wanted to stay until the transfusion was over, but my dad insisted that he would be fine and told her to go to the party so that she could give him a full report of the festivities, detail by detail.

After the celebration, we drove my mom home. We all gathered around the dining room table, called my dad, and put him on speaker phone. It was just the five of us: my mom, Bob, Tracy, Jason, and me.

We told my dad that we had a birthday cake for him right there at the dining room table. We lit the candles and sang happy birthday. Afterward, we gave him a blow-by-blow of the party. He sounded great. We were relieved that the transfusion went well, and he was awake and jovial as always. We assured him that we would all be at the hospital to visit him first thing in the morning.

My dad wanted to know who would be staying with my mom that night. My mom told him that Tracy was spending the night with her, and that Jason was spending the night with Bob and me. I remember him saying, "Good, that's good."

Just before we got off the phone I said, "I love you, Dad." Little did I know that would be the last I'd ever talk to him.

Not even thirty minutes later, my mom received a call from the hospital saying Dad had passed away. His eleven-year battle with prostate cancer had ended. All five of us immediately drove to the hospital feeling devastated. I was upset with myself that I hadn't been there with him when he died. It was one of the worst nights of my life.

Losing my dad was the hardest thing I had ever been through. My kids and I were all trying to be strong for my mom, but we were all dealing with our own grief.

My father left behind a legacy of humility and service. He fought for civil rights for his friends and neighbors. Sitting back and watching the segregation and unfairness was not an option. In 1968 he fought for the Fair Housing Act and worked with Burbank Temporary Aid to help African Americans and Hispanics find places to rent or buy in our local community. He also brought the religious leaders of our community together to improve neighborhoods, create friendships, and embrace differences. He encouraged people to learn from each other rather than judge one another.

My father was also dedicated to Jewish education. In memory of his friend Morrie Rosen, my dad set up a scholarship fund to provide financial aid for families who couldn't afford to send their children to Jewish summer camp and Hebrew School.

My children both have their grandfather's philanthropic heart. For many years, Tracy has been involved with organizations that help underprivileged and abused children. Through her art gallery, she also started an art scholarship for high school students who wish to further their education in the arts. After the Woolsey Fire in 2018, Tracy opened a free shop for people who had lost their homes in the fire. She was able to gather enough clothing and shoes to help many of the residents who had lost everything.

When Jason was in his mid-thirties, he lived in San Diego and developed a special connection with the elders in his community. He "adopted" one older lady in particular, who was about eighty-five years old. He mowed her lawn and planted flowers in her garden at no charge. He also brought in her groceries and served her meals. After learning that she loved spaghetti, Jason would often cook her a big batch of spaghetti and bring her several serving-size containers that she could store in her freezer. She once asked Jason for my phone number. It was a sweet surprise to receive a phone call sharing that my son was taking such good care of his "San Diego Grandmother." I made it a point to visit her when I went down to see Jason in San Diego.

For many years, Jason managed an apartment complex that housed many college students. A lot of these kids were broke and living off of Top Ramen. Jason regularly BBQed and fed them his famous fish tacos. To this day, he always looks out for those who are in need.

Mom

After my dad died, my mom stayed active for a couple of years until her health started failing. She stopped driving and became sedentary. It took great effort to get her out of the house, even to visit the synagogue. Then she developed Alzheimer's and rapidly started losing her memory, to the point where she had forgotten she had a second daughter. My mom and Cele had become estranged over the years, so when Cele died in 2006, the doctor advised against telling my mom. Mom passed away in 2008, at the age of ninety-four.

I was so proud of my mother for accomplishing all that she had. She was forty-five years old when she went back to school. She graduated from the University of Judaism with a permanent teaching certificate. She also received an associate of arts degree from Los Angeles Valley College, and a bachelor of arts degree from the Hebrew Teachers College. After earning her teaching credentials, she taught Hebrew School for approximately ten years and later took the librarian position at the University of Judaism. She enjoyed learning how to use a computer at around sixty years old. She, too, was granted many merits and awards from her community. Her dedication to Jewish education and Jewish life was impressive.

My parents kept a Kosher kitchen, and it was especially important for my mom that she pass on all of our family traditions and recipes to my daughter. Tracy has the same passion for keeping tradition. My mom was thrilled that Tracy would come for a week at a time during the holidays, especially Passover, to help her bring out the dinnerware and prepare the food. To this day, Tracy still uses the same Passover dishes and Seder plates that we used at my parents' house for sixty-six years. She also uses the crystal that my parents received as wedding gifts in 1935. About a year before my mom died, Tracy moved in with her to help me care for her.

My mom loved my kids. She was always so grateful when they came to visit. She was especially happy when Jason would drive up from San Diego to stay for a few days. She always had Jason's favorite chocolate cake waiting for him. When Jason was attending the University of San Diego, he bought a school sweatshirt for my mom. She always made sure she was wearing it when Jason came to visit. She treasured her time with him.

While my parents were still alive, I didn't feel comfortable devoting a lot of time and effort into searching for my birth mother. Even though my parents are the ones who suggested I look for her after my migraines started, I still worried about hurting them. After my mom died, however, I felt open to taking more aggressive steps. But I had no idea where to start. I felt that I didn't have the money it would take to hire a private investigator. Plus, I didn't have a name or much helpful information to give the investigator. Back then, online tools for finding family weren't as popular or well known.

Getting Closer

Several years later, however, in January 2015, I saw an ad on television for 23 and Me, the DNA testing website. It reminded me that Linda had joined about six months earlier and was thrilled to discover cousins she never knew she had. I said to myself, *You know what? I'm just going to order the DNA kit!* I didn't really expect to find my birth mother on 23 and Me. At that point she would have been eighty-five years old, and I doubted she had joined. But I thought I might find siblings or other family members.

About eight weeks after I sent in the kit, I received the results with the percentages of my ethnicity. Not surprisingly, given my red hair and blue eyes, I found out that my ethnicity estimate is 46.5 percent British and Irish, 31.4 percent French and German, 16.4 percent broadly Northwestern European, and 3.3 percent Scandinavian. Later I joined

Ancestry.com, and according to my DNA test with them, my ethnicity estimate is 71 percent English, Welsch, and Northwestern European; 25 percent Irish and Scottish, and 4 percent Swedish.

There was also an option on 23 and Me to find my closest DNA relative, so I did. The website notified me that I had been matched with a possible second or third cousin with the initials JW, but it didn't say which side of the family.

In early April 2015, I contacted JW through the 23 and Me website. I mentioned that I was not sure how we were related. She responded a few days later and said that I matched some other relative matches she had received. JW also asked, "What's your number?"

"What number?" I messaged back.

"Your GEDMatch number," JW responded. "If you upload that number on the GEDMatch website, we might be able to figure out how we're related. It shows you the relatives that you share the most DNA with."

She also asked where I was adopted so we might be able to narrow down the ancestors we had in common. I sent the nonidentifying information I had received from the Department of Social Services.

After JW mentioned the GEDMatch number, I found mine and visited the GEDMatch website, but I couldn't figure out how to use it. I went to Linda's house and we spent hours trying to navigate the website, but it was not very user friendly. I let JW know that we were having a hard time finding information, but I didn't hear from her again.

In May of 2015, Linda invited me to attend a three-day genealogy seminar in Burbank. She knew of my ongoing search and thought I might be especially interested in hearing the keynote speaker. Local newscaster Chris Schauble, from Channel 5 News, was sharing his story of how he found his birth family. Like me, Chris hadn't known where to begin his search, so he hired a private investigator. The investigator did a ton of legwork, flying back and forth across the country, chasing down leads. He was extremely lucky to get Chris's adoption file unsealed. It took the private investigator quite a while, but he finally located Chris's birth mother, sister, and brother. The investigator also learned that Chris's birth father had passed away.

Chris was able to meet his brother first, and later he met his birth mother and sister. He had such an emotional reunion with his newfound family. His birth mother, sister, and brother were all thrilled that he found them. Chris was even able to find answers for some medical issues he had been having.

Chris's story had many ups and downs, and it gave me hope of finding my own birth parents. I really wanted to ask him some questions. Unfortunately, partway through his talk I became so overwhelmed with emotion, wondering if this could happen for me, that I started to develop an intense migraine. It felt like hot steam was rising from the top of my head. After the talk, the pain was so intense that I could barely speak to Chris when I went up to thank him for sharing his story. Chris's private investigator, Jay Rosenzweig of JR Investigations, was there. I briefly spoke to him and got his business card, and then I found Linda. "You have to get me home right now," I said.

I spent the next three days in bed with a migraine and couldn't attend the rest of the seminar. I was so disappointed. I really wanted to hear the other keynote speakers and get other ideas about finding my birth family. Hearing how the investigator had gotten Chris's records unsealed and found his birth mother gave me hope. But I wasn't sure if it would ever happen for me.

Just one year later, however, a door opened and my life changed forever.

PART III:

Finding

Chapter 7:

Mary

"SUE, TURN ON THE LEARNING CHANNEL!" Linda said as soon as I answered the phone. "*Long Lost Family* is on. You have to watch it!"

I had never heard of the show, but I immediately turned it on. The series was about adoptees searching for their birth parents and/or birth parents searching for the children they had given up for adoption. In that episode two separate families were reunited. I couldn't stop crying during the show, and I just kept thinking how I wished that could be me.

I decided it was time to try again. If these people found their families, maybe I could, too.

It had been about ten months since I attended the genealogy seminar where I heard Chris Schauble talk about his journey to find his birth family. Over those months, I kept thinking about how Chris found his family. He had hired a private investigator who had flown all over the country tracking down family members. I guessed that investigator had cost Chris at least $50,000, and I didn't have that kind of money. So, in those ten months, I hadn't moved forward in my own search.

The next day, I called Linda and asked her if I could come over and have her help me write some letters. Linda is a genius with correspondence and getting to the point succinctly. I knew that she could help me construct the various letters I wanted to send. We spent several hours writing letters to everyone we thought could help me get more information about my birth mother. In the end, we wrote fourteen letters. I was so grateful for Linda's help.

First, I wrote to the son of the doctor who delivered me. My amended birth certificate doesn't indicate the place (i.e., hospital) of birth, but it does list a doctor's name. Unfortunately, the doctor had passed away, but I located his son, who was living in Northern California. In my letter I asked three specific questions: (1) Do you know what hospital your father was associated with in 1947? (2) Was your father associated with any homes for unwed mothers at the time? (3) Would he have had an association with an attorney specializing in adoption at that time?

The son emailed me within a few days. He gave me the name of one hospital where his father worked in the 1940s. He also said he was unsure whether his dad had delivered babies at a home for unwed mothers. I contacted the hospital that he mentioned, but they no longer had records from 1947.

Next, I wrote to the adoption records department of the Adoption Unit at the Edmund D. Edleman's Children's Court in Monterey Park, California. I requested all the forms needed to unseal my adoption records. I figured the restrictions might have changed since I first visited the Los Angeles Superior Court in 1965. Unfortunately, they hadn't, and I still couldn't access my records.

Linda wrote a lengthy letter to a local adoption attorney, asking about the possibility of getting my records unsealed. He replied with his fee and a few more details. Linda gave me the info and said, "Let's just call him."

The lawyer was straightforward on the phone. "My fee is a flat $1,500, but I would just be taking your money. The judge who hears these cases is a real tough cookie. You would need a letter from two different doctors, one being a psychiatrist, saying you are obsessed with finding your birth mother. Unless you can prove that you are obsessed, that you don't eat, you don't sleep, you've got psychological problems, it's very difficult to get this judge to unseal those records. I'm telling you right now, I don't think she's going to do it. She's very, very tough."

"But I'm sixty-eight years old!" I replied. "Who am I hurting?"

"I know, but I also know that judge. Your best bet might be to contact a private investigator." I appreciated the lawyer's honesty, but it was still hard to hear.

I also contacted several television personalities who had been adopted. First, I wrote to Chris Schauble and thanked him for sharing his story at the genealogy seminar. I also asked him for suggestions on how to get my own adoption records unsealed. He suggested that I contact Jay Rosenzweig, the private investigator who helped him. I didn't think I could afford to hire Jay, so I didn't follow through.

I wrote two separate letters to the two cohosts of Long Lost Family. I told them what information I had and asked if they had recommendations for getting my records unsealed. In response, I received a letter from the Learning Channel saying that they would contact me if they were interested in featuring my story on the show.

I wrote to a former CNN anchor who shared her adoption story on television. As with the other two TV personalities, I asked her for suggestions. She provided the names of a couple adoption websites that I could join. Shortly after receiving her response, I joined Booth Baby Adoption and Adopted.com and wrote letters to both organizations. I also sent a letter to the Alma Society, which I had joined back in the 1980s. Unfortunately, none of these sites got me any closer to finding my birth mother.

Around the same time that I wrote these letters, I joined the International Soundex Reunion Registry, which tries to unite adoptees with their birth parents. The registry also helps birth parents seeking information on the children for whom they made adoption plans decades earlier. I filled out the application in hopes that a family member might be looking for me.

Because a hospital wasn't listed on my amended birth certificate, I thought I might have been born in a home for unwed mothers. I searched homes for unwed mothers in Los Angeles around 1947 and found two: St. Anne's and Florence Crittenton Center. I wrote letters to both. St. Anne's was now a Social Services organization operating as a maternity home. Someone responded to my letter and said they no longer had records from 1947. I also heard back from the Florence Crittenton Center and learned that the center was now a charter school. The person who contacted me told me the records from the 1940s were stored in the charter school's basement.

"The corporate office is coming out soon to remove all the records and take them to another site," the lady told me. "You're welcome to come down and go through them. Can you get here in the next few days?" I made an appointment with her to go there on the following Monday. Talk about perfect timing!

Bringing in the Experts

After writing all of those letters and receiving no new information, on March 28, 2016, I finally decided to contact JR Investigations, the firm that had helped Chris Schauble. I was so nervous. Even as I dialed, I was thinking, *I don't know if I can do this.* I couldn't believe that Jay himself answered the phone.

After I explained why I was calling, Jay asked me what information I already had.

"No identifying information," I replied. "But I have a name bracelet that says M Francis. And I found a second or third cousin through 23 and Me, but I have no idea if the person is on my mother's side or my father's."

"Well, that information could be promising."

"Great! How much is this going to cost me?

"It's $795."

"That's it?! What are the additional charges?" I thought a big shoe was about to drop.

"There are no additional charges."

"Really? That sounds *great!* What's next?"

"Go to our website at BirthParentFinder.com and fill out the application. My associate Diane will follow up with you in a few days."

I thanked him profusely and got right to work. I jumped on the website and filled out the application. I was so excited, and I couldn't wait to get the journey started.

I didn't have to wait long for a response! About three hours later, Diane emailed me, thanking me for reaching out. She asked if I had requested nonidentifying information from the state. "Also, please let us know if you've taken a DNA test with any of the major companies offering them today, such as Ancestry or 23 and Me."

I emailed Diane right away and told her the little I knew about where I was born and what doctor may have delivered me. I also told her what I had learned from the adoption attorney, that I would need a "compelling reason" to get my records unsealed. I shared that I had joined 23 and Me but didn't understand how to use the GEDMatch number.

Diane's response was very encouraging: "We do not ever rely on a judge's order to open a sealed adoption file. It just does not happen … The good news is that we do NOT need to open your sealed record in order to find your birth mother. We can locate your birth mother (and any other children she may have had) simply through your nonidentifying information." That was *great* news!

This was the first time I had considered that I might have siblings out there. I felt overwhelmed, in a good way. This was becoming more real and more exciting. I felt like I was *finally* going to get some answers.

I immediately paid the $795 and made it official. I had hired people to help in my search! This felt too good to be true, but I was more hopeful than I had been in all of my previous attempts.

Diane had explained that the first step would be to track down my birth mother's maiden name. "We have a source who will look up your current amended birth cert and get the numbers off of it," Diane wrote in an email. "She'll then go into the microfiche to scan it and search for the matching record. This record will be your original birth record with your birthmother's maiden last name (ONLY) on it." This sounded promising! I couldn't sleep that night, just thinking about the possibility.

The next day, however, Diane called. "Well, I don't know if I can help you because I don't have records going back to the 1940s. Mine only go to the 1950s. But I have a DNA expert in New York who is very good. His name is Dave. Do you want me to talk to him for you?"

I said of course, and I also gave Diane my 23 and Me password so that Dave could see what information I received, including the genome number. Diane told me he would know how to use that number.

On Sunday, April 3, Diane emailed with an update from Dave. By logging into my 23 and Me account, he could see the second cousin match, though at this point he couldn't tell what side of the family JW was on. He could also see I had not downloaded my raw DNA data from 23 and Me. He was able to do this for me and then send it to GEDMatch. He told Diane, "It will take a day or two for the results to appear, but what this does is compare her DNA to persons from all three tests [23 and Me, FTDNA, and Ancestry] that have uploaded their raw data to GEDMatch." One comment in particular gave me hope: "I do think this is solvable with the DNA." *It's happening*, I thought. *It's really happening!*

Diane closed that email by saying, "You probably won't hear from Dave or I until those results are in … prob by Thursday." My heart raced at the possibility that Dave could actually find my birth mother that week. Talk about being on pins and needles!

Success

On Monday, April 4, Bob and I drove to the Florence Crittenton Center in East Los Angeles to see if we could find my records. We were met by two very nice ladies at the front desk. The one I had spoken to on the phone remembered me, and she escorted us downstairs to the storage room.

We then entered a dark and dingy basement, where an old walk-in refrigerator was being used to store files. When she opened the door to the refrigerator, I gasped. Inside, boxes and boxes and boxes of old, musty records were stacked floor to ceiling and about forty rows deep. Some boxes were labeled but most were not. The sight was overwhelming. I was also bewildered that this gal who didn't know me was allowing us to search through boxes of confidential records. It made me feel a little uneasy.

Bob and I took down a few boxes and started looking through them, but we didn't see anything labeled 1947. In fact, we didn't see anything labeled earlier than the 1960s. After half an hour or so, I looked at Bob and said, "There's no way the two of us can do this. This is an impossible task. We would have to come back with an army of people, and even then, we might not find anything." It was discouraging to say the least.

We decided not to keep searching. We thanked the women for helping us and said good-bye.

I arrived back home very disappointed. I guess I had envisioned going through labeled boxes and miraculously stumbling upon information about my birth parents. The truth was, I would probably never find my records among the thousands in that walk-in refrigerator, especially not if I only had a couple days before they were being removed.

There was a message on my answering machine, so I hit play.

"Hi, Sue. This is Diane. Call me as soon as you get home. I'm in a meeting, but call me." The urgency in her voice made my head spin.

My hands shaking, I picked up the phone and dialed Diane's number. She answered.

"Sue, I think we found her," Diane said.

I nearly dropped the phone, and then I started sobbing. My heart was racing.

"Is she alive?" I asked.

"I'm not sure. Give me another hour. I'll call you back."

For that next hour, I felt like I was going to have a heart attack, which wouldn't be good because I had hoped that I would be alive in sixty minutes to take that call! Bob tried to get me to relax, but nothing worked. He even poured me a glass of my favorite wine. It was delicious, but it did nothing to calm my nerves.

Waiting for that call was the longest hour of my life.

I had had so many conversations in my head about what I would say to my mother if I ever found her. I had dreamed this dream a thousand times. And, now, I might just have that chance.

An hour later Diane called. "Sue, she's alive."

"Oh my God! Where is she?"

"She lives in a very small town in Upstate New York."

"But, she's alive!

"Yes, she's alive."

After fifty years of wondering and searching and hoping, my dream had finally come true. It is impossible to express the overwhelming joy I felt at that moment.

Later that day I checked my email and found a message from Diane. She had forwarded the email from Dave in which he realized he had found my birth mother.

Using the nonidentifying information I received from the Department of Social Services, the name on the beaded bracelet, the genome number, and my match to JW, Dave went to work. He researched newspapers in Upstate New York for obituaries, wedding notices, and more. He found one article from a small-town newspaper in Steuben County, which is near the New York–Pennsylvania border. "As you know," he wrote to Diane, "JW, Sue's second cousin match, had ancestry from Pennsylvania and Chemung County. Chemung County is adjacent to Steuben County."

He went on to quote the newspaper, which said, "Miss Ruth _____ of Wellsboro, Pa., is a guest of her aunt, Mrs. Donald Francis and family." He also attached a clipping from a 1947 newspaper in the same small town, which described the wedding of one Barbara Francis, who was one of Ruth's cousins.

He then wrote, "Oh my God, we have them! Sue's birth mother's Father was 47 years old in 1947. He completed high school. He was a manager at a feed store. Sue's birth mother's Mother was 43 years old in 1947. Her birth mother had two brothers and two sisters! The birth mother is MARY FRANCIS!! That was what was on Sue's beaded bracelet, M FRANCIS!!!"

Reading those words gave me chills. In just three days, he had accomplished what I couldn't in fifty years. Using my genome number and my second or third cousin match, he was able to piece together the fact that JW was somehow related to a woman named Ruth, who was my birth mother's cousin.

I didn't know what to do first. I couldn't wait to tell Bob and the kids.

Making Contact

The next day, Diane called. After we chatted for a few minutes, Diane asked, "Do you want me to try to contact Mary?"

"Yes," I replied without hesitation. "I would appreciate it if you would contact her." I didn't think I could do it. I was too nervous, scared, and overwhelmed to even think about talking to her on the phone. I just knew I would fall apart.

When Diane called Mary, she reached her voicemail. She left a message saying, "I'm a genealogist/private investigator doing some research on your family name. I would appreciate it if you could call me back."

About a week later, Diane had not heard back from Mary, so I decided to write to her myself. I carefully constructed the following letter and sent it with a few pictures:

April 12, 2016

Dearest Mary,

I hope that this letter finds you well.
My name is Susan Shurman Hurst. I am 68 years old.
I was born on May**, 1947 in Los Angeles, California.

I was adopted at just three days old. I was wearing a beaded bracelet with the name "M Francis."

I have kept this bracelet my whole life in hopes of finding you.

I was able to receive some information from the Department of Social Services. This information stated that my biological mother was 16 at the time of my birth. It stated that her father was the Manager of a Feed Store and that her mother was a housewife. My mother had two brothers and two sisters. The information also stated that my biological father did not know of the pregnancy, nor the birth. It also stated that he was a US Marine and that he was 20 years of age at the time of my birth.

I believe that you are my mother!

Morris and Rose Shurman, my adoptive parents, were loving and kind people, who gave me a perfect and charmed life.

I was reared in Burbank, California, where I still reside. My parents have since passed away but had encouraged me to search for you.

Being a minor at the time you delivered me, my birth records, with your identification, were sealed.

After many, many years, my search has finally come to fruition.

I have a wonderful husband, two beautiful children, and a gorgeous two-year-old granddaughter, who are the loves of my life.

I understand that privacy may be an issue, and I respect that, but I have been searching for you and loving you my whole life.

My birthday is in a few weeks. The best gift that I could possibly receive would be the chance to finally meet you.

Again, I understand if privacy is an issue as you may not have shared the information of my birth with your family.

I truly hope that you will consider meeting me. I will gladly, excitedly, and joyfully fly to New York in a HOT NEW YORK MINUTE, just to realize this dream come true. I found you! I'm overjoyed and overwhelmed. I cannot explain it all in this short letter.

I hope and pray that you will feel the same way.

I will anxiously wait to hear from you in any way that is most comfortable for you.

Sincerely and with love,
Susie (M Francis)

I have enclosed a picture of my beaded bracelet, a picture with me and my mom, and a recent picture (two months ago) of myself and my daughter Tracy.

The beaded bracelet

Me and my mom, 1950

Me and Tracy, 2016

About two weeks went by without a response from Mary. I knew the letter had been delivered because I received delivery confirmation. I had included both my cell and home numbers, my home address, and my email address. I was confused as to why she hadn't responded. I started worrying that Mary was ill and in the hospital. Or maybe she was simply away on an extended vacation. I couldn't consider the possibility that she didn't want to know me.

I went on Ancestry.com to see if I could find out if my birth mother and her husband had any children, but I couldn't find any information. I emailed Diane to see if she could help. Diane emailed back saying she found one possible child named Terri. She thought it was our best bet as far as any children. She told me she would try and figure out what Terri's maiden name was.

Sure enough, Terri had the same last name as my birth mother. Diane asked if I would like for her to contact Terri.

"Yes, but if she doesn't answer, don't leave a message," I replied.

As it turned out, Diane got in touch with Terri on the first try. Terri was driving when Diane called, so she pulled over to the side of the road. Diane gave her an abbreviated version of my story—that I had taken a DNA test and I believed Terri's mother was my birth mother.

Diane contacted me the next day to tell me about her conversation.

"Oh my God, how did it go?" I blurted out. "What did she say?"

"Terri would like to talk to you," Diane told me.

"Really? Oh my God!" I couldn't believe it. I had a sister *and* she wanted to talk to me!

"She just said to give her a couple days to talk to her mom. She didn't seem too surprised. She actually said she always thought her mom had a secret. By the way, Terri is adopted, too." I was surprised to hear that!

I called Tracy right away. Jason was living in Bangkok, so I emailed him right afterward. I didn't want to wake him up in the middle of the night but, I just *had* to tell him!

A few days later I received an email from Terri introducing herself as T.K., for Terri Kaye. "My mom is Mary Francis," T.K. wrote. "She is the woman you sent the letter to."

I was so overwhelmed with joy. I was so elated that my sister was reaching out to me, and I responded immediately. I asked about Mary's health. "I have been very worried about her," I told T.K. "I hope my letter didn't upset her too much. I tried my best to let her know that I was coming from a place of love and understanding."

"Yes, she is all right," T.K. responded. "I would love to talk to you! As you know I was also adopted, but there is another daughter, Kim, who was not adopted, and she also would love to meet you."

She included her phone number and asked me to call her that Sunday. I actually had *two* sisters who wanted to meet me!

When I phoned T.K. on Sunday, I found out that as soon as she hung up with Diane a few days earlier, she had called Kim, and the conversation had gone something like this:

T.K.: "If you're not sitting down, you need to."
Kim: "Of course I'm sitting down, I'm driving home."
T.K.: "Mom did have a secret. She had a baby when she was sixteen and never told anyone. A genealogist just called. We have a sister!"
Kim: "Oh my gosh!"
T.K.: "Do you believe her?"
Kim: "Of course, I believe her. Why would she make it up?"

The girls decided to go talk to their mom that night. T.K. bought the biggest bottle of wine she could find. Then she picked up Kim, and they drove straight to Mary's house. Apparently, the conversation didn't go well.

T.K. and Kim chatted with their mom for a little bit and then T.K. asked, "Mom, did you get anything important in the mail?" Mary said she didn't think so. T.K. tried again. "So, you didn't get a letter from California?"

About that time, Mary's face went white, and she told her daughters, "They promised me no one would ever know."

She admitted that she gave a baby up for adoption and then told her daughters, "This is the only time I will talk about this. Don't ever bring it up again." Mary thought that I had somehow had her records unsealed, and she was very upset that her secret was out.

The girls tried to convince Mary to call me or to write me back, but she was very reluctant and didn't promise anything.

In my conversation with T.K., she apologized for her mother's response. She also emphasized that she and Kim wanted me to come visit.

Then T.K. said, "I want you to know there is another sister. Mom was unable to get pregnant for ten years, so my parents adopted a baby girl and named her Susan."

I was dumbfounded to learn that she was unable to conceive after all those years, but even more by the fact that she named her daughter Susan! Was it a coincidence? Or did Mary see the name my parents gave me when she signed the adoption paperwork? I'll never know, but I like to think she named her first adopted daughter after me.

"Kim and I decided not to tell our sister about you," T.K. said, interrupting my thoughts. "She always resented the fact that she was adopted. We don't think she would take it well."

"I understand," I replied. "Don't give it a second thought." But I kept thinking about the fact that I had a sister named Sue!

T.K. admitted that she had looked through my photos on Facebook. In fact, Kim had done the same thing! The next day, I received a beautiful email from Kim:

I'm so excited to know that my family has just grown! I want you to know that I welcome you with open arms. It is still somewhat shocking, but in a very good way. I have looked through your pictures and you have a beautiful family. I am looking forward to finding out all about you and all of them.

I was overwhelmed with emotion after reading those words. I forwarded the email to Tracy, and then replied to Kim. I told her how grateful I was to be welcomed into their family. I also mentioned that I wanted to fly to New York on the weekend of June 10. "It is my daughter, Tracy's, 50th birthday," I told Kim. "This would be such a special way for us to celebrate her birthday, with our growing family."

Kim was overjoyed at the prospect of Tracy and I coming to visit. She told me that I would be able to meet her family as well as some cousins. I was beyond thrilled.

I also talked with T.K. about our potential visit. She and her husband own the Colonial Motel in Watkins Glen, a bed and breakfast that is about five minutes from her house. She offered to let us stay there. T.K.'s daughter and son-in-law were going to be visiting her that weekend, and they wanted to meet us too. Again, I was so overwhelmed by the generosity and love from these people I hadn't even met. I was reeling with emotion.

The day after T.K. and I emailed about our accommodations, I came home from the market as the mailman was approaching. We had a short, friendly conversation as he handed me the mail. I turned and walked into the house. Just inside the door, I leafed through the envelopes and froze when I saw a letter from Mary. My hands started to shake. I was excited and nervous all at the same time. I had to leave in a few minutes for my first day on a new job, but I couldn't wait until I got home. I stood by the front door, opened the envelope, and read the following:

Dear Susan,

I am very upset that you called my daughter. My girls did not know about you and I did not want them to. Do I want to meet you—no, I do not. Please love your family as I love mine.

I am sending you a picture of my mother, myself and grandson, taken 35 years ago. I am now 85.

Mary Francis

Her words cut me like a knife.

I read the letter several times to make sure that I read what I thought I had read. How could this be true? I wondered how she could be so upset and not want anything to do with me. This is the woman I had been searching for my whole life. I had put her on such a pedestal. I had been dreaming of this day for the last sixty years. I was devastated.

I wanted to climb into my bed, bury myself under the blankets, and cry my eyes out. I couldn't do that. I had to pull it together and go to work. But I didn't think I could do it.

At first, I didn't tell Bob about the letter. I didn't tell Tracy or Jason either. I just couldn't share with them what Mary had written. It was too devastating. My heart was broken and my dream of a happy reunion had been shattered, but I didn't want them to feel sorry for me.

I needed someone to pull me out of this nightmare. The only person I could think of was my friend, Annie, because she always makes me laugh. Thankfully, Annie answered the phone. After I told her what had happened, she said, "Susie, don't cry. It's her loss. She doesn't know what she's missing." And then Annie did what she does best: she made me laugh.

Annie and me, 2016

By the time I got to work I felt a tiny bit better, and I was somehow able to make it through the day. On my way home, I started thinking about the letter again. I got so upset that I developed a raging migraine. When I got home, all I could do was lie down. I eventually fell asleep, and when I woke up my migraine was not nearly as bad.

Later that evening, I emailed T.K. and Kim. I told them that I had received a response from their mother, and I told them what she had written. I asked them not to mention the letter to their mom, or the fact that I was in contact with them. I thought it would just make it worse.

Later that night T.K. and Kim both responded to my email. They told me they were so sorry for their mom's response. They also reassured me that they were so glad I had contacted them. "Please find comfort in knowing we can't wait to meet you and Tracy," T.K. wrote. And Kim said, "T.K. and I are so excited that you have come into our lives."

Even though the response from Mary was not what I had hoped it would be, I felt so grateful that I had gained two loving sisters, something that I had always wanted. My sisters were as anxious to meet me as I was to meet them.

Chapter 8:

Pat

I HAD WRITTEN to the Department of Social Services (DSS) in 1993 and received some nonidentifying information about my birth parents. After watching *Long Lost Family* in March 2016, I decided to write the department again, just in case they had any new information. I also mailed a "Waiver of Rights to Confidentiality for Siblings" form, so any siblings I might have could contact me if they wanted to.

I didn't hear back from the DSS for eight weeks. By that time, the investigator had already found Mary, and I had already been communicating with T.K. and Kim. Although the DSS letter didn't provide any identifying information, it did give me a few more details about my birth father and the events surrounding my actual birth.

May 16, 2016

Dear Ms. Hurst,

This letter is to inform you that we have received your request dated March 14, 2016, for copies of your adoption file. Unfortunately, we are unable, by law, to provide a copy of your adoption file to you.

We have also received your Waiver of Rights to Confidentiality for Siblings form and a second Consent for Contact, and have placed them in your adoption file. The California Department of Social Services (CDSS) may release names and addresses to an adult adoptee (18 years of age or older) and a birth parent only if each has signed a Consent for Contact form. We may also release names and addresses to siblings, 18 years of age or older, who have been separated by adoption only if each has signed a Waiver of Rights to Confidentiality for Siblings form. Siblings under the age of 18 years may also complete a Waiver of Rights to Confidentiality for Siblings Under the Age of 18 form with the consent of their parent or guardian. The CDSS will provide consistent and waiver forms only upon request, as soliciting consents and waivers is prohibited. To date, we have not received any other consents, waivers, or inquiries.

Regarding your request for non-identifying information about your birth parents, enclosed is a copy of the report previously sent to you on March 29, 1993. We have not received additional information since then. However, the following is supplemental information that may be of interest to you.

To hide her pregnancy from neighbors and friends, your birth mother and her mother came to California from New York to live with your birth mother's older sister until you were born. They told others that they made the trip for an extended visit with her older sister. They stayed in California approximately 4 months. When your birth mother returned to New York she hoped to finish school.

Your birth mother signed a consent to your adoption on May 14, 1947. Your adoption was finalized in Los Angeles County Superior Court on November 19, 1947. The court action number was AD-*****

Your birth mother's oldest brother was married, lived in New York, and worked at the same feed store as their father. Her younger brother was 14 years old and was a student. Her oldest sister lived in California and worked for a telephone company. Her other older sister lived in New York and also worked for a telephone company.

Your birth father's brother was older than he was, was married, and was in the U.S. Navy. His oldest sister was married, his next older sister was a nurse, and his younger sister was still in school.

Your birth parents knew each other for about 5 years before she became pregnant. Your birth father's name is on your original birth certificate.

Please be advised that in the future, you may simply write a letter if you need to update your contact information or make an inquiry. There is no need to have your signature notarized or witnessed by a representative of the CDSS each time.

Our records indicate that you previously petitioned the superior court pursuant to Health Safety Code Section 102705 (formerly 10439), and we provided a copy of our file to the court on July 13, 1993. You can refile a petition in an attempt to obtain additional information about your adoption as indicated below:

- **Original Birth Certificate**—You may attempt to obtain a copy of your original birth certificate by petitioning the Los Angeles County Superior Court or the superior court in your county of residence under California Health and Safety Code Section 102705. You will need to provide good and compelling cause for the granting of that order. It will be at the discretion of the judge as to whether the original birth certificate will be unsealed.

- **Court Documents**—You may attempt to obtain documents (relinquishment or consent, adoption decree, etc.) from the court file by petitioning the Los Angeles County Superior Court under California Family Code 9200. It will be at the discretion of the judge as to whether any documents will be released to you.

You may contact the superior court where your adoption was finalized at the following address and phone number to obtain more information about this process:

Los Angeles County Superior Court

Children's Court Adoptions Unit

201 Centre Plaza Drive, Room 2100

Monterey Park, CA 91754-2158

(323) 307-8099

www.lasuperiorcourt.org

If you have any questions, you may contact _____ at (916) 651-8094 or by mail at 744 P Street, M.S. 8-12-31, Sacramento, California 95814.

As happy as I was to receive this "new" information, it wasn't new at all. Clearly it had been sitting there in my records all along when I had asked for this information twenty-three years earlier. I wondered why now they had a little bit more to disclose.

After receiving this letter, I began wondering how I could find out more about my birth father. Although his name was on my birth certificate, I couldn't get my birth certificate unsealed to view the name. I also knew that I wasn't going to get any information from Mary. I asked Diane if she could help me find my father, but she said without a name she didn't know where to begin. With Mary, I at least had a name bracelet and a connection through my DNA test. With my dad, I had nothing.

When I received that letter in May 2016, I was working for my friend Jane, taking care of her mother. One day Jane and I took her mom to a doctor's appointment. As we sat in the waiting room, I told Jane about the recent letter from the DSS, and the new information about my birth father.

When Jane got home later that day, she started thinking about how we might be able to find my father's name with the little information I had. Jane guessed he had to be someone who lived close to

Mary because they had known each other for at least five years and her hometown was small and somewhat isolated. Social circles were fairly localized in those days.

Jane took on the role of detective and set out to find my father. First, she gathered the basic information we had received from the DSS. We knew that at the time of my birth, my father was a Marine, his father worked for the government, and he had one brother and three sisters. We also knew the birth order and occupations of his siblings and the fact that Mary had lived in Steuben County, New York. Using this information, Jane set up search parameters on MyHeritage.com to look through the 1940s census records.

First Jane put in "Steuben County," "Marines," "male," and a birth-date range of 1928 to 1930. We received hundreds of possible names in response. The list was organized by head of household. It included the head of household's first and last name and occupation, followed by the names and ages of the spouse and children. In those days census records were handwritten, and some of the names were hard to read. We felt like we were searching for a needle in a haystack.

Jane and I divided up the pages of names and started eliminating people who didn't fit my father's family profile. For example, if we saw there was a husband, wife, and only one child, we crossed them off and moved on to the next name. If we found a family that seemed to have the right number of children in the right birth order, we wrote down the names and then researched those names online to see if we could narrow down the ages and professions of each sibling in 1940. This was a very long and arduous process.

After a few weeks, we still had no luck in finding a family that seemed to fit. On the Saturday before Tracy and I were to leave for New York, Jane called me and said, "Tell me again what the letter from the Social Services told you."

I read her the whole letter.

"Oh, I think I have the siblings in the wrong order," she said.

Jane started all over. She generated a new list using the same parameters and went through it looking for families with the right number of children in the correct birth order. Then she entered those names one by one into the computer.

One day after going through pages and pages of names, Jane decided she was just going to do a few more before calling it a day. Just before she was going to stop, she entered one more name, and all the stars aligned. His father was listed as mail carrier, which is a government job. One sister was a nurse. One sister was a student. His parents were about the right age. His family lived in the same town in Steuben County. But Jane didn't want to say anything to me in case it was the wrong family.

On the Monday before Tracy and I left for New York, I was at Jane's house taking care of her mother. Jane came home from playing golf and we chatted for a few minutes. Then Jane said, "Sue, I think I found him!"

"Oh my gosh. Are you sure?"

"I'm 99 percent sure."

"What's his name?"

She told me his first name was Lyman, a name I had never heard before. I eventually found out he went by his middle name, Pat.

I was so elated and called Tracy on my way home from Jane's.

"Tracy, we may have found my father!" I said as soon as she answered.

"Oh my God!" Tracy replied.

We weren't 100 percent sure, and we were leaving for New York in a couple of days to meet my new sisters, so I decided to put my father on the backburner for a while. Tracy and I agreed that we wouldn't say anything to T.K. and Kim, not until we were sure.

New York

Tracy and I were so excited to meet our new family and wanted to look our absolute best, so we both got a manicure, pedicure, and obligatory spray tan (it was June, after all). We also bought new clothes and had our hair cut.

Unfortunately, that plan backfired. I felt like I needed a change, so I told my hairdresser to give me a shorter haircut. However, I realized too late that I don't like short hair on me.

"Well, I just have to buy a wig!" I told Tracy. I hadn't done that since the 1970s!

Tracy and I visited the closest wig store. As we parked the car, I said, "I think Raquel Welch has a wig line!" and we started laughing before we even walked in.

Tracy pulled every red wig off the mannequins, and I tried them all on. Tracy even tried on a few. We couldn't stop laughing. We finally found one that was closest to what my hair looked like before the haircut. Sold!

Before heading to New York, Tracy and I devised a plan. After our plane landed, we would get our rental car, have a bite to eat, and then take a nap. We were going to spend the night in Buffalo, visit Niagara Falls, and then head to Steuben County the next day to see my family and visit the historical society to do more research.

When we arrived in Buffalo, we grabbed our luggage and headed down the escalator toward the car rental area. We were exhausted from the red eye and were dying to check into our hotel room and get some rest.

As we neared the bottom of the escalator, I saw three people smiling and waving at us.

I recognized my sister right away. "Oh my gosh, it's Kim!" I said to Tracy.

As soon as we stepped off the escalator, Kim gave me a huge hug and said, "We couldn't wait until tomorrow to meet you! We just had to come and meet you when you got off the plane." The tears were pouring down our faces.

The airport was about 150 miles from Kim's home. I was so touched that she made the trip to come meet us. It was the best surprise.

Kim introduced us to her son, Logan, and her cousin, Connie. They were so lovely and just as excited to meet us as we were to meet them.

The three of them went with us to get the rental car. While we were waiting in line, Connie asked me if I knew who my birth father was. Tracy blurted out, "Does the name Pat _____ mean anything to you?"

I stared at Tracy. We had agreed to not say anything until we were 100 percent sure, but it just happened so spontaneously with Connie asking.

Kim answered, "Yes, I know who that is."

"I think he might be my birth father," I said,

"What? He and his family lived four doors down from us when we were growing up," Kim said.

"No way!" Tracy and I both said.

"Yeah," Kim said. "I dated his son Chris for like five minutes in high school. I made out with him in our basement!"

"I remember making out with Chris, too!" Connie said.

We all laughed hysterically.

Tracy shared that we had recently received some information that indicated that Pat was most likely my birth father. We filled them in on what Jane had uncovered, and it all made so much sense. From there we began comparing notes. It was so overwhelming that Tracy and I became increasingly tired. We all went to get something to eat, and then

Tracy and I needed a nap! Kim, Connie, and Logan ended up getting a hotel room right next to ours, so they hung out while we slept.

When we woke up, Tracy and I hurried downstairs to meet everyone in the hotel lobby. We decided to visit Niagara Falls together since it was on our list of things to do. On the way there, we acted like tourists and made many stops to take pictures, including a hotel with a sculpture of the Blues Brothers.

Tracy (far left), me, Kim (standing behind me), Logan, and Connie

Niagara Falls was breathtaking, and we took hundreds of photos, maybe even close to a thousand. We had a great time and the conversation was filled with talk about our lives over the last fifty years (except for Logan, who was only twenty). We all had so much to say and so many questions to ask one another. After hours of walking and talking, we worked up quite an appetite, so we headed to a nearby Italian restaurant and had a wonderful dinner together, laughing and chatting. I felt so comfortable with my new family and didn't want the evening to end, but we were all exhausted from the travel and excitement.

The next morning, we got on the road early because we were so anxious to get to Kim's house in Steuben County. When we stopped for lunch, I mentioned that I needed to use the restroom. I jokingly said, "I have three kidneys, so I have to stop a lot!"

"Maybe you can give Mary one of your kidneys if she needs it. She's on dialysis," Connie replied. I was surprised to hear that Mary and I both had issues with our kidneys.

"Well, if she's nice to me and wants to meet me, I will happily give her one of my kidneys!" We all laughed.

After lunch, we got back on the road. Kim had a little surprise for us. She wanted us to meet her oldest son, Mike, and his daughter, Abby, so we headed to Mike's new house. It was really wonderful how my sister was so open to introducing us to her family. It was completely unexpected, since she didn't really know us at all.

We stayed for about an hour and played with Mike's adorable baby girl. When we left, Connie jumped into our rental car so that we wouldn't get lost on the way.

When we pulled into Kim's driveway, her husband, Dave, was standing there waiting for us. He wasn't smiling. When I walked up to give him a hug, he initially took a step back. He was clearly uncomfortable and was stiff as a board when I wrapped my arms around him.

Tracy recognized his apprehension and said, "Can you believe this crazy story? This is something you only see on *Primetime* or *Dateline!*"

"I'm not going to lie to you," Dave said. "I have a gun in my pocket! How do I know why you're here, standing in my front yard? Anyone can look you up on the Internet. How do I know you're not trying to get something out of Mary?"

Being the comedian that she is, Tracy said, "Well, what kind of a gun are you packin'?" Dave pulled a very small caliber gun out of his pocket.

Tracy laughed and said, "Are you kidding me? Look at me! That little gun isn't going to do any damage to a girl like me! I was expecting at least a 357 Magnum!"

He then dropped the clip out of his gun and showed her the hollowed-out bullets! Tracy high-fived Dave and said, "Now, that's impressive!"

Then Tracy said, "Well, I'm not gonna lie to you! I thought that maybe you were going to bury us in the cornfields. I thought that maybe you would bury us like Mary has been burying this deep, dark secret for sixty-eight years!"

That did it! That broke the ice. Dave welcomed us into his home and brought us straight into his man cave and gave us a tour. At that point I knew we were all going to be friends.

Kim needed to take care of some things around the house, so Connie decided to take us on a little journey on our way to T.K and Paul's bed and breakfast.

As we drove, Connie said, "I'm going to show you guys some-thing!" She told Tracy to pull over and then said, "Get out of the car."

"Why are we stopping here?" I asked. We were in a parking lot in the middle of nowhere.

"See all those vineyards over there?" Connie said, pointing to the lush and serene view to the right and left. "Our grandparents used to own those vineyards."

It was an incredibly beautiful sight, and I was touched that she said *our* grandparents. I felt so loved and welcomed, and I had only known Connie for twenty-four hours.

After we looked around and took loads of photos, Connie had us drive to her house so we could meet her boyfriend, Ben. They live in a charming log cabin in the most beautiful area in the mountains. Bears come right up to the front door. Ben has a recording studio there and he gave us a tour. He told us that the Red Hot Chili Peppers had recorded there.

After a short visit, we headed to the bed and breakfast. T.K. greeted Tracy and I with big hugs and kisses. She showed us to our rooms, which were so charming. We shared a Jack and Jill bathroom. Tracy's room was full of flowers, a bottle of champagne, and a few birthday cards from our new family members. They really rolled out the red carpet.

After we showered and changed our clothes, we headed downstairs and found that T.K. and her husband Paul had brought in a delicious BBQ dinner. Also, we were surprised to meet Connie's sister, Cheri. To celebrate Tracy's fiftieth birthday, T.K. and Paul had a three-layer chocolate cake and some cupcakes, and the hotel band played music and sang happy birthday. We couldn't believe how thoughtful and generous my new family had been.

After celebrating and singing and having a few glasses of wine, I became exhausted and decided to go to bed. I wanted to stay up and continue to party with everyone, but I was worn out. Kim, T.K., Connie, and Cheri took rooms at the hotel, so they decided to have a slumber party with Tracy. They chatted until the wee hours of the morning.

When I woke up the next day, I started to develop a headache, due to all the excitement. But, damn it, I had to put that wig on! My head hurt so bad. I didn't think I could do it.

"Mom, you are going to look like a kook if you go down now, without that wig. You have to put it on!" I tried, but I couldn't do it. My head hurt too much, and the wig seemed to be tighter than ever!

So, we strolled downstairs and told my family the story of my very short haircut, and we all laughed.

T.K.'s daughter, Heather, and her husband, Brad, had driven up from Manhattan for the weekend and we had a lovely visit. Heather was pregnant with their first child. As soon as we started chatting, they mentioned that they were taking a trip to Thailand before the baby was due. We told them that my son, Jason, moved to Thailand in 2010 to teach English and that now lives there with his lovely wife, Nana, and their daughter, Naiya Rose, who is the love of my life. (They did end up meeting Jason and had a wonderful time!)

After breakfast, the group decided to go on a hike in Watkins Glen State Park. T.K. and I stayed behind, since we hadn't had much time to visit with one another. T.K. was so easy to talk with, and there was never a lull in the conversation. We talked and laughed like we had known each other our whole life.

After a few hours, everyone returned from the hike. I was still a little tired, so Tracy went to T.K. and Paul's house with Brad and Heather, so that I could nap and they could get to know each other better.

Connie, Cheri, and Kim also went back home. Kim's son, Logan, was leaving for college soon, and she was helping him get ready. Connie and Cheri had some things to do to prepare for the BBQ that Connie was hosting for us the next day.

At six o'clock there was a knock on my door. T.K. brought Tracy back to the hotel and brought me a gluten-free dinner. The three of us ate in the room and talked for hours. It was perfect. We didn't want our evening to end.

The next morning, T.K. surprised us once again, this time with hot tea, a basket of muffins, fruit, and a load of goodies. I had the most thoughtful sister! She made me feel so special.

After breakfast, Tracy and I decided to check out the quaint little neighborhood while everyone else was doing their Sunday morning rituals. T.K. told us about a little restaurant where Mary and her friends go after church, and she thought we might like to take a sneak peek. I had previously sent Mary a letter with a photo of Tracy and myself, so I didn't think it would be a good idea. I didn't want her to recognize us and become upset.

When we walked downstairs, we saw Paul in the kitchen. We told him we were going into town for lunch and shopping. We asked if we could bring him anything.

"Would you mind helping me in the kitchen?" he asked. "I'm making ice cream."

"We would love to!" we said.

So, Tracy and I cut up Reese's Peanut Butter Cups and Oreo cookies for his homemade ice cream—and we ate about a hundred dollars' worth of candy while chopping! We still made sure to leave plenty of room for the final product and ate about fourteen scoops of ice cream later that day. We had a great time bonding with Paul, talking and laughing. Tracy and I both felt that Paul looked like Peter Fonda, so that's what we nicknamed him.

Afterward, Tracy and I went shopping at an antique store before heading to my cousin Connie's for dinner. While there, we found an old wooden artillery box that would be perfect for Dave's man cave. We also bought him a few NRA pins, since he's such a gun enthusiast.

Of course, we also bought a few things for ourselves. We found an old compass from WWII that Tracy bought for her husband, Jeff. She put it in a box with a card that read, "Thank you for being my North, South, East and West."

When we arrived at Connie and Ben's house, Dave was sitting outside. In front of him on the table sat two cans of corn and two of his pistols—corn because we initially joked about him burying us in the cornfields. Tracy and I presented Dave with the artillery box, and he was so touched that he got tears in his eyes. We also gave him the NRA pins, and he immediately put them on his T-shirt.

Connie knew that I have many dietary restrictions, so she prepared a steak just for me without any seasoning. She pointed out to everyone, "This steak is for Sue. No one is to touch it!" Connie also had a special salad for me, and she remembered that I like Fritos, so she had some in a bowl on the table. I was so appreciative of the extra effort she put in.

Before we sat down to eat, Paul offered to call Mary and tell her that they were having a little get together at Connie's house, and that he would go pick her up and bring her over. I said, "Please Paul, that wouldn't be right. I think Mary would be devastated that you all knew about me. I appreciate the offer, but I think it would be extremely hard for her."

During dinner, Dave told me he was sorry I didn't get to meet my mother.

"You know, I had a great mother and father," I said. "Mary gave birth to me, but meeting all of you and having you accept us the way that you have … I couldn't ask for anything better."

Then Connie stood up and said, "I want to propose a toast." She then looked at me with tears in her eyes and said, "Susie, thank you for your persistence, your tenacity, your time, and your energy. We are so glad that you found us. We love you and Tracy so much." Tears streamed down my face and Tracy's. We had all bonded in an amazing way, even though I didn't know these people existed two months earlier. I can't explain how much it meant to me that everyone was so lovely, warm, and inviting. These people were my family, and I loved each and every one of them!

During dinner I was chatting with Connie about family history and our ancestry. She told me she had the lineage records for Mary's family going back several hundred years.

"Would you like a copy?" Connie asked.

"I would love it. That would mean so much to me," I replied.

After dinner, she began to photocopy pages and pages of documents. I was so thrilled. In the end she gave me around fifty-five pages of our ancestry, including pictures of Mary, her parents, and her sisters and brothers. Connie also had pictures of our great-grandfather's barbershop from 1906 and the family's Wholesale Grocery Store from 1913. I was fascinated at all the information that she had on *our* family. I was also fascinated that she had records going back to the 1700s from Norwich, Norfolk, England. *Now I know why I am 52 percent British*, I thought.

While Connie was photocopying these pages, we started drinking the wine that Tracy and I had brought. We were all laughing and getting a little tipsy, when out of nowhere, Connie asked, "Hey, do you want to meet my mom?" Tracy and I had heard Connie say that her mother had passed a few years ago, so we were a little confused.

Then she walked us into her pantry and opened a drawer. *What the heck is she gonna pull outta this drawer?* I wondered.

Connie pulled out a sippy cup and said, "Say hi to Mom!"

We almost spit out our wine. It was too funny!

That incident just confirmed that these were our people! They were straight-up, fun-loving, crazy people with a fantastic sense of humor. Connie was about to put her mother back in the drawer when Tracy said, "Whoa, stop right there. She has to stay for the party!" We couldn't stop laughing.

When we got ready to leave Connie's house, Tracy and I said our good-byes. We knew we weren't going to be seeing Connie, Cheri, Ben, Kim, or Dave before we left in the morning to fly home. I hugged everyone for the longest time and didn't want to let go.

Tracy and Dave singing at the BBQ

In the back: Tracy, Kim, me, Ben, and Connie.
Middle: Paul and T.K. Front and center: Cheri.

Me hugging Connie, not wanting to let go

After dinner, Tracy and I went back to the hotel. I sat on the edge of my bed and thought, *If I die tonight and don't wake up, this was the best day of my life.* I felt so happy and content in this town, in the countryside, and with my warm and welcoming family. I wished that we had more time to spend with everyone. I didn't want to leave them and go back to California. I had never seen such beautiful country. I felt like I belonged here, where my family lived.

Later I called Bob and told him, "I love it here. It's so hard to leave my family. I just found them, and now I have to leave." I started to cry, not knowing how soon I would see them again.

In the morning, T.K. came over to say good-bye and to help get us back on the highway to head to the airport. We hugged for the longest time. I didn't want to let her go. All three of us were so emotional. Luckily, Tracy was going to drive. I felt so exhausted, but a good exhausted.

On the long ride back to the airport, we made a list of all the fun nicknames we gave to our fun family. We started with Dave. We called him "KoRnNutz" because we thought he was going to bury us in the corn fields. Tracy named my sister Kim "Auntie Kiki." Paul was "Peter Fonda," for obvious reasons. Cheri we named "Brass Knuckles" because she played several brass instruments. Connie we named "Triple C" for our Crazy Cousin Connie. Logan was "Lo Man." It just went on and on. We had so much fun with them.

There aren't enough adjectives to describe our unbelievable new-found family.

Back Home

A few weeks after our trip to New York, I wrote back to Mary. I thanked her for writing and for sending the beautiful photo. Then I told her the real reason I was writing for a second time.

Dear Mary,

I am writing to you to see if you could find it in your heart to share some family medical history with me. I would be eternally grateful.

A few years ago, my daughter, Tracy, became very ill and almost died. She was hospitalized several times. The lining of her kidneys was disintegrating, and her entire body was suffering and went into ketosis. I remember the doctors asking me for our family medical history. As a mother it was very painful and excruciating for me to see my child suffering. Unfortunately, I had to tell the doctors that I had no family medical history on my mother's or father's side because I was adopted.

My daughter suffered horribly. She was unable to eat or sleep. She became extremely depressed and lost about 60 pounds. She was skin and bones.

I decided that it was time for me to begin my search again for my birth parents. I kept hitting a lot of roadblocks, which was extremely disappointing and frustrating.

Not until this year, did I join a DNA website to see if I possibly had any birth relatives. I also hired a private investigator.

I want to apologize for upsetting you in any way. That was certainly not my intention. The private investigator contacted Terri, not me. I am just searching for medical history for myself, my daughter, Tracy, and my son, Jason. All three of us suffer from horrible migraine headaches, where we sometimes lose our peripheral vision. I also have what is known as painful bladder syndrome, and I, like my daughter, have issues with my kidneys. I have also had 12 skin cancer surgeries.

Again, I am sorry for any pain I may have caused you.

I'm just a mother searching for answers for her children, their health and well-being.

I wish you only the very best.

Sincerely,
Sue

To my surprise, Mary responded about two weeks later:

I have very little information for you. My daughters are healthy with no problems. I have no information on the birth mothers. They always say, "Mom, you are my mother." I am 85 years old, in good health. Ten years ago, I had a heart attack, and have a pacemaker. I do have a kidney problem and have been on dialysis for four years, and do very well.

I hope your family is doing better.
Mary

I was so thankful she wrote back, though I was hoping for a little more information.

After we returned from New York, I also did more research on my birth father and his siblings. I continued looking through the 1940 census records, and I joined Newspapers.com and Whitepages.com to see if I could find more confirming evidence. Jane also continued searching on MyHeritage.com and other websites.

Everything about Pat's family lined up with the information I had received from the DSS. By July we determined, without a doubt, that Pat was my birth father. Unfortunately, we had also learned that he had passed away in 2003. I was devastated that I would not be able to contact him or possibly have a relationship with him.

Through our research, we learned that he had four children, one daughter and three sons. From an obituary notice for Pat's wife, we learned the names of all four children. To my amazement, his daughter's name was Susan! *Oh, my gosh*, I thought. *Three sisters named Susan!*

I again wondered if Mary ever told Pat about me. I also wondered if she knew I was named Susan. If so, did she share that with Pat? Of all the names he and his wife could have come up with—I couldn't believe they chose Susan.

With the names of all Pat's children, we began to search for possible phone numbers. We ran into a lot of dead ends. Most of the phone numbers we found were landlines, and by 2016, many people had gotten rid of their landlines so it was hard to find a valid phone number. Jane finally found the number of a Jennifer who appeared to be the daughter of Pat's middle son.

I went to Tracy's house on a Sunday morning in August 2016 and had her call Jennifer because they were close in age. When Tracy called, Jennifer answered. Tracy asked if she was Pat's granddaughter. When she said yes, Tracy said, "Jennifer, this is going to be the craziest phone call you will ever get."

Then she explained who she was and who I was, and that we believed that Pat was my birth father, and said, "We're 99.9 percent sure your grandfather had a child in 1947 that he didn't know about. I know this is a lot to ask and you don't know us, but we're wondering if someone from your side of the family would be willing to submit a DNA test.

We'll pay for it, and you can check us out to make sure we're not crazy people. We'd just really like to know if Pat is my mother's birth father."

Tracy read all the information about Pat that we had, and Jennifer kept saying, "Yes, that's him. Yes, that's him." Jennifer confirmed that her father was Pat's son. At the end of the call, Jennifer said she would drive over and talk to her dad and then call us back.

Again, I was on pins and needles waiting for a return call. Sure enough, Jennifer called back about an hour or two later.

"My dad isn't interested in talking to you," Jennifer said, "but you can call my Aunt Susan. Just give her a couple days to process all this before you call."

"Oh, that's great!" Tracy said. "And we are both on Facebook, if Susan wants to look us up."

I was disappointed that I had a brother who was not interested in talking to me, but at least I had a sister. I waited a couple days and then I called Susan. From the first few words out of our mouths, we had a connection.

I told Susan that I found Mary through 23 and Me. I said that if she wanted 100 percent confirmation, I would pay for the DNA test. I told her I was not some crazy person, that I just really want answers. I have been searching for so long now, and I'm so close.

"No DNA test needed," Susan said. "You're my sister. I always wanted a sister, and now I have one!" Susan had looked at my Facebook profile and could see the family resemblance.

I was so thrilled to hear her say those words, "No DNA test needed." I thought, *Yes, I have a sister, and she said that she always wanted a sister, too!* Plus, we both had the same name! I now had three fabulous sisters.

Susan and I talked for quite a while. She said she would send me pictures of *our* dad. She also said her youngest brother, Chris, wanted to ask me some questions. I was a little leery about calling him. I was afraid he was going to ask me things like "What do you want from me and my family?"

I called Chris the next day and it turned out that he just wanted to know if I had any questions for him about our father. He shared some stories about our dad, and we had a lovely conversation.

I asked Chris if he wanted me to pay for a DNA test, but he said no. He believed me. He, too, had looked me up on Facebook and saw a striking family resemblance.

Pat's other two children weren't interested in connecting, but that was okay. In Susan and Chris, I had two more siblings that I never even knew I had. I felt so blessed. I finally had a brother. I wished he would have been around to protect me when I was growing up with Cele.

Susan told her son, Bryan, and her daughter, Heather, about me. We texted each other a few times. Bryan and Tracy even spoke on the phone once, and the call lasted a couple of hours. Bryan told Tracy that his wife was "freaking out" because, he never talks on the phone, and certainly not for that long.

A few weeks later Susan sent me a picture of our dad in his Marines uniform. My father looked exactly like my son. The resemblance was uncanny. I immediately sent the photo to Tracy and Jason. Tracy said, "No DNA needed."

Jason couldn't get over the resemblance either. Every single inch of their faces was identical, from the hairline, to the jawline, lips, mouth, nose, and eyes. It was surreal. I never thought that I would find my birth father, so seeing these images side by side left me speechless.

I sent those pictures of Pat and Jason, side by side, to everyone in the family. They couldn't believe how identical they were. Susan's daughter, Heather, even said, "Oh my God, they look like twins."

After I received my birth father's picture, I pulled out my senior high school photo and did a side-by-side comparison between Pat and me. *Now, I know where I come from*, I thought.

Left: Jason in his early twenties, around 1990
Right: Pat at age eighteen, around 1946

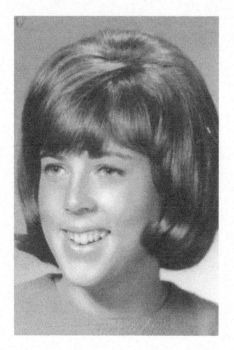

My senior picture, 1965

Chapter 9:

The Story of Pat and Mary

FOR CHRISTMAS 2016, I sent gifts to my newfound siblings. I gave T.K., Kim, and Susan a Christmas ornament in the shape of a star. It read "Sisters are like stars. They make things brighter." My brother Chris is a huge New York Yankees fan, so I sent him a Yankees baseball cap.

I also received some lovely gifts from my siblings. Susan's present in particular caught me by surprise: she sent me a framed picture of my birth parents as teenagers from the year 1946, along with a note that read, "If you ever had any doubt about your mom and dad, this should answer it." Pat and Mary were standing in front of their high school, looking obviously comfortable and familiar with each other. Susan's husband Jerry had been down in the basement looking for pictures of their grandkids when he came across this photo. They never knew they had it.

Pat and Mary, 1946

Finally, I had a picture of Pat and Mary together! I never dreamed a picture of the two of them was out there somewhere. I was so grateful to Jerry for uncovering this jewel. Based on that photo, I was pretty sure Pat and Mary had been an item! This made me so happy. This was the best gift I could have received.

Now I wanted to know more about Pat and Mary and their relationship, so I started searching.

Mary

Mary was born in Upstate New York in September 1930, and she lived there her entire life. Mary's grandparents owned vineyards, which stayed in the family for many years.

According to the information I received from the Department of Social Services, Mary was musically inclined, and she enjoyed singing. In high school, she participated in the dance committee, she was a class officer, and she also played varsity basketball.

Mary and Pat grew up in the same small town and went to the same schools, although he was two grades ahead. They most likely met at school, and at some point, they started dating. Around August 1946, just before her junior year of high school, Mary became pregnant. She was fifteen years old at the time. About a month later, Pat joined the Marines. He left for boot camp in October 1946 without ever knowing he was going to be a father.

I have so many questions about what happened around this time. Did Mary know she was pregnant before Pat enlisted? Did Pat write to her while he was gone? If he did write, did Mary write back?

I do know that at some point at the end of 1946 or beginning of 1947, Mary and her mother travelled to California to stay with Mary's oldest sister until I was born. According to the letter I received from the Department of Social Services in 2016, Mary and her mother left New York to hide Mary's pregnancy from friends and neighbors.

If Pat was writing to Mary, did her dad tear up the letters that Pat sent while she was in California? She had no way of knowing where he was stationed, so even if she wanted to, she couldn't have written to him from California. How hard was that time for both of them? Was Pat still in love with her? Was Mary in love with him? Did Mary's parents forbid her from ever seeing him again? So many unanswered questions.

Mary gave birth to me on May **, 1947. Twelve days later, Mary signed a consent to my adoption. Shortly thereafter, Mary and her mother returned to New York.

In the fall of 1947, Mary started her senior year of high school. She worked at a movie theater as an usher and in the concession stand. She continued to be highly engaged in school activities. She was also named prom queen. In the spring of 1948, Mary graduated from high school.

In the fall of 1948, Pat returned from his two-year stint with the Marines. At some point, he and Mary reconnected. I located a gentleman named Jesse, who had worked at the winery with Pat many years later. He told me that after Pat returned from the Marines, he had proposed to Mary, and she turned him down. During her senior year, Mary had met a young man named Alfred, and it is possible they were already dating when Pat returned and proposed.

If Mary and Alfred weren't dating in late 1948, they began seeing each other shortly thereafter. Soon they were engaged, and they married in June 1950.

For a period after the wedding, Mary worked as a bank teller. She also worked as a secretary for the Code Enforcement Department.

After trying unsuccessfully for ten years to have their own children, Mary and Alfred adopted a daughter in 1960 and named her Susan. In 1962, Mary and Alfred adopted their second daughter, T.K. Surprisingly, Mary got pregnant a few years later, and gave birth to my sister Kim in 1965.

Mary and Alfred raised their kids in the same small town where they grew up. Mary was a stay-at-home mom who was active in the community and in the local Methodist church. Her husband owned a successful business that enabled his family to enjoy a comfortable lifestyle. They were avid golfers and belonged to the local country club. They also traveled a lot for Alfred's business.

In the early 1970s, the family decided to move to a different part of town, but the house they moved into wasn't the house that Mary really liked. She had her eyes on the beautiful brick home across the street. After a period, that house came on the market and Mary and Alfred bought it.

Low and behold, Pat and his family, lived four doors down the street, and they had lived there for years before Mary and Alfred moved in. Why did Mary want to live on that street? She must have known that Pat lived there. Was she secretly still in love with him? What torture for both of them.

My sister Kim remembers hanging out with Pat's son Chris, who was around her age. She said that whenever Chris came over, Mary was never nice to him. I wonder how she felt when Kim and Chris dated for a short time.

Kim also remembers that Pat never drove past her house, even though that was the shorter route out of the neighborhood. He would deliberately drive the longer way, presumably to avoid seeing Mary and Alfred. I think it was just too painful for him to catch a glimpse of her. I truly believe that Mary broke his heart when she didn't accept his marriage proposal. I am a hopeless romantic, and I think she was the love of his life.

Because it was a small town, Pat and Alfred had connections too. In fact, they had probably known each other their whole lives. They had been in Boy Scouts together and had both received a service medal. They also worked at the local post office together in the early 1950s, around the time they both got married. I think it must have been exceedingly difficult for Pat, having to work alongside Mary's new husband. Maybe Pat was upset that Alfred had started dating his girl while he was away in the Marines. I honestly believe that he was crushed.

Alfred died in 2005. Mary stayed in the same house where she raised her kids, and then moved to a retirement community around 2010.

By the time I found Mary in April 2016, she was in the beginning stages of vascular dementia. She had also been on kidney dialysis for approximately four years because she had a rare kidney disorder. Kim believes her mom would have come around and accepted me if I had found her before the dementia developed, but I'll never know.

In February or March 2018, Mary stopped going to dialysis because she didn't think it was helping. After that, Mary's condition steadily declined. Kim and T.K. kept me updated on Mary's condition, and I debated about going out to visit. However, I didn't want to upset Mary. She only had a limited amount of time left, and I felt I needed to do what was best for her. Plus, if she became angry at my presence, I would have been even more brokenhearted. The whole situation weighed on me heavily. Then Mary developed fluid around her heart and lungs, and in April 2018, she passed away. It was almost two years to the date after I had found her.

I didn't attend the funeral because I didn't want to take a chance in upsetting family members who didn't know about me. I sent a wreath of flowers from our family, and I sent Kim and T.K. my love, but I decided it was best if I stayed home. It was a difficult decision. I had searched for Mary my whole life, and even though I found her, I still never got to meet her.

I still have mixed emotions about not going to see her while she was in the hospital. I really wanted to give her a big hug and to thank her for giving me life, but I didn't want to cause her any emotional pain. As much as I wanted answers to my many questions, I also wanted her last days to be peaceful, so I let her go to the grave with her answers.

After Mary's passing, I still wanted to investigate her life. I joined Classmates.com to try to find any of Mary's classmates who knew about her relationship with Pat. I attempted to contact about fifty people from her class. Only a few people were still alive. One lady remembered Mary and told me they were on the basketball team together in high school. However, she didn't have any other information. The other ladies I spoke with didn't have any information either. After using Classmates.com, I went on Whitepages.com in my attempt to find some living classmates. It was terribly sad to discover how many had already passed away.

When I was younger, I hoped that Debbie Reynolds was my birth mother. What an unbelievable coincidence that her given name was Mary Frances, and my birth mother's name was Mary Francis.

Pat

My birth father was born in Upstate New York in March 1928. He was the fourth of five children. He had two older sisters, an older brother, and a younger sister. Pat grew up in the same town as Mary, where his father was the Postmaster General and his mother was a homemaker. His ancestors go back to Kilkenny County, Ireland. I always thought I might be part Irish, with my red hair, blue eyes, and freckles.

Pat was an athletic young man. In high school, he was on the tennis, basketball, baseball, track, bowling, wrestling, and football teams. He graduated from high school in June 1946.

The following September, Pat joined the Marines and left New York in October. By that point, Mary was pregnant, although she may not have known she was, and Pat definitely didn't know. He spent two years in the Marines. His release date was August 26, 1948. He returned a few months after Mary graduated from high school.

My sister Kim recently told me that there is a signature in Mary's yearbook that reads:

To Mary

That California Gal

Pat

I'm not sure if this Pat was my dad, and I'm not sure if he ever knew she went to California and why. Maybe it was just a girlfriend of Mary's named Pat. I will never know.

Sometime after Mary rejected Pat's proposal, he started dating another girl, whom he married in April 1950—a few months before Mary married Alfred. Pat and his wife were married for approximately twenty-five years and had four children—three sons and a daughter named Susan. I like to think Pat knew about me and that my name was Susan. I like to think that he had a say in giving his daughter the same name. I will never know.

After Pat returned from the Marines, he worked for the US Post Office. Around 1952, he started working at a local winery, and continued working there for the next twenty-five or so years.

Pat and his wife eventually divorced. Pat remained in the same area afterward.

As I had with Mary, I looked up Pat on Classmates.com and wrote down all the names of his classmates in his senior year. I reached out to approximately forty to fifty people. I also looked up the name of the winery where he worked. Then I went on Newspapers.com and found articles that discussed the twenty- and twenty-five-year commendation awards he received from the winery. The articles also gave the names of other employees who had received awards. I wrote down all the names and attempted to call each one of them, about forty to forty-five people total.

One gentleman named Walter, who worked with Pat at the winery, told me that Pat was a good fella and a hard worker. He also told me that Pat used to take a nip now and then, as did some of his coworkers. I thought it was hysterical that Walter shared that with me.

I spoke with another gentleman, Paul, who said that he and Pat both owned 1957 Chevys. He told me that Pat's was two-tone blue, with dark blue on the bottom and a lighter blue on the top. I was thrilled to hear that, since my mom used to have a '57 Chevy and I still love those cars. Paul didn't have any information about Pat and Mary's earlier relationship.

In his later years, Pat had a daily habit. He would drive to a little country market to buy a banana and a slice of pumpkin pie. The problem was that he always parked in the fire lane.

Well, it just so happened that one of the police officers in that small town was Pat's very own granddaughter, Heather. On more than one occasion, when the police were called to give Pat a ticket, Heather was the one who responded to the call.

When the station was phoned, one of the officers would find Heather and say, "Hey, we just got another call from so and so market. It's your grandpa again." If Heather was available, she would take the call.

She had to explain to her grandfather that he couldn't park there, but he never understood what the trouble was all about. Every time it happened, he asked her, "What's the big deal?"

Pat was eventually diagnosed with bladder cancer, and he died in 2003.

I truly regret that I was never able to meet my birth father. In my heart, I feel that we would have enriched each other's lives.

I have always loved traveling to the wine country in Northern California, and I find it remarkably interesting that both of my birth parents had deep connections with vineyards. Mary's parents owned vineyards for years, and Pat worked in a winery for over twenty-five years. I often wonder if my birth parents walked hand in hand among the vineyards in their small community. I'd like to think that they did.

I have tried to contact over 150 people to find out more about Pat and Mary. Of the dozens I interviewed, no one could tell me about their relationship, with the exception of the man who told me that Pat had asked Mary for her hand in marriage. Was their relationship a secret? What was life like in the 1940s in their small town? So many unanswered questions.

Chapter 10:

The Siblings I Always Wanted

SHORTLY AFTER TRACY AND I RETURNED from New York in June 2016, I received a card from my sister Kim that read, "It's hard to believe that six months ago I didn't know anything about you and now I can't imagine not having you in my life. Thank you for never giving up!!"

Kim's words made me feel so loved. Even though Mary didn't welcome me with the open arms as I had hoped, Kim and T.K. had. I'm also grateful that Pat's children, Susan and Chris, have welcomed me unconditionally. As a child, I had always wanted a sister to share secrets with and a brother to protect me from Cele. And now I had this, and so much more.

The Perfect Birthday Gift

I turned seventy in May 2017. Tracy and her husband, Jeff, invited Bob and me to their home in Malibu to celebrate. We were going to have lunch and then walk along the beach so I could collect shells. Tracy knows that this is one of my favorite things to do.

As soon as Bob and I arrived, I used the restroom. When I came out, I saw my sister Kim sitting on the couch. I couldn't believe it. I immediately started to cry. We gave each other a huge hug and didn't let go of each other for some time. We both had tears in our eyes, as did Tracy.

"What are you doing here?" I cried.

"You can thank this one, right over here," Kim said as she pointed to Tracy. "I got in last night. Tracy flew me in to surprise you!"

Tracy invited T.K. as well, but she was unable to make it.

The five of us went to lunch at my favorite seafood restaurant. Afterward, we all went for a walk on the beach. It turns out that Kim loves walking along the beach and collecting shells as much as I do.

Me, Tracy, and Kim on the beach in Malibu, 2017

Later, Kim gave me a birthday present. It was a necklace with a pendant of grapes growing on a vine with an emerald, my birthstone, set in the middle. Kim had it made just for me, because she wanted me "to have a piece of home." The grapevines represent the vineyards our grandparents owned. It was so special. Her thoughtfulness overwhelmed me. Of course, I wear my necklace every day!

That night everyone drove back to our house. We enjoyed a wonderful dinner together and sat around the pool in our backyard for hours, drinking wine, talking, and laughing. Bob had a fire going in the fire pit, and we told stories all night long. The next morning, we had breakfast by the pool. Kim was happy the weather was warm, unlike New York at that time. She loved sitting outside in the morning sun, and I was thrilled she was there.

After breakfast, Tracy, Kim, and I drove back to Malibu. Kim and I took another stroll on the beach to collect more shells, while Tracy ran some errands. We took a few more pictures. Later that evening, Tracy made a delicious dinner for all of us. Unfortunately, Kim's visit was brief, and after dinner, Tracy and I took her to the airport so she could catch the redeye back to New York. At the airport, we hugged each other for a long time. I didn't want her to go.

Me and Kim collecting shells in Malibu, 2017

I couldn't thank Tracy enough for making my seventieth birthday so special. The memory of that weekend will always be a special one.

Not long after that, Tracy and Jeff flew to Manhattan for her friend Brad's wedding. They arranged to have lunch with T.K.'s daughter Heather; her husband, Brad; and their daughter, Mya. They had a great time.

Jeff, Brad, Heather, Mya, and Tracy, 2017

Back to New York

I returned to New York in June 2017, and this time Bob came with me. We stayed with T.K. for the first two nights so we could visit with T.K. and Kim and their families. The first night we met Kim, Dave, Logan, and Logan's girlfriend, Morgan, for a beautiful dinner on the lake.

The next day we went to Watkins Glen State Park for a picnic with Kim, Dave, T.K, Connie, Ben, and Cheri. We went on a short hike, and I was able to see the beautiful gorge. We then came back to our campground, and Dave barbequed hot dogs and hamburgers. We played games, ate, drank, and had the best time. The next day we took a cruise on the lake, taking in the breathtaking surroundings. I still cannot get over what a beautiful part of the country my family live in.

A couple of days later, Bob and I went to visit my siblings on Pat's side of the family. First, we drove to my sister Susan's house. Although I had spoken to Susan and my brother Chris, I had never met them. I was so nervous. We had had wonderful conversations over the phone, but what would it be like in person?

Me, T.K., and Kim, 2017

As soon as Susan opened the door, we both started crying and we hugged each other tightly. A few minutes later, Chris arrived and gave me a huge bear hug. I felt so welcomed by this side of my new family as well.

We all went out to the patio in the backyard and relaxed. I brought out my gifts for Susan and Chris. I gave Susan a box of See's candy, which she had never tried because they don't have See's in their neck of the woods. It turns out her favorite piece of candy is the same as mine: scotch mellow. Of all the different kinds of candy in that one-pound box, Susan likes the same kind I do. Of course, she does!

I gave Chris a 1962 New York Yankees yearbook with Mickey Mantle and Roger Maris on the cover. "Where did you get this?" he asked with tears in his eyes. "Do you know how much this is worth?"

I told him I really didn't know what it was worth.

"Well, what I have for you is nothing compared to this," he said.

"I'm sure it will be," I replied. And I was right.

Chris brought out an envelope and handed it to me. Inside was Pat's high school varsity letter for football, basketball, and baseball. He also gave me a patch from our dad's US Marines uniform and an artillery casing from the twenty-one-gun salute at Pat's funeral. I couldn't believe his generosity and the fact that he wanted me to have these items that he had for so many years. The fact that he was giving me these precious items meant so much.

Pat's high school letter, a patch from his Marine's uniform, and an artillery casing from the twenty-one-gun salute at his funeral

Susan, Chris, and me, 2017

I had brought lots of my childhood photos to share, so that we could look at photos of each other growing up. Susan shared several photos of herself, our dad, and lots of family. She also gave me lineage information about Pat's ancestors. I was thrilled. She then handed me an envelope. Inside was a booklet that Susan's husband, Jerry, had put together. Jerry had taken Pat's senior yearbook to a printer and had them make copies of every page that featured Pat. On the front of the booklet was the same picture of my birth mother and father in front of the high school, and next to the picture was Mary's signature: "Love, Mary."

Then Jerry and Susan showed me the original yearbook, and the only signature in the entire book was Mary's. I was shocked. He was so popular in high school and played every sport imaginable, so I was expecting hundreds of signatures, but he only had one—from Mary!

That signature made me think that maybe they really did love each other.

A few days later, I took the yearbook back to my sister T.K.'s house and asked Kim, T.K., and Connie if that was Mary's signature.

"Yes," said Connie. "I used to forge that signature all the time!" Whenever Connie and Kim cut class, Connie would forge Mary's name.

After the gift exchange with Susan and Chris, my new family took me to the VA cemetery where Pat is buried. When I came upon his headstone, I started to weep. I kissed the headstone, and Susan laid a wreath she had made in front of it. The cemetery grounds were impeccable. I was quite impressed.

My sister Kim works at the VA hospital, so we stopped by to say hi after we visited the cemetery. Kim knows Susan and Chris from when they used to live down the street from each other in the 1970s. Kim also used to work with Jerry. We then visited the Catholic cemetery where other members of Pat's family are buried. It was overwhelming seeing all the family headstones from the late 1800s and early 1900s.

That evening, Susan's daughter, Heather; her family; and Chris's wife, Julie, came over to Jerry and Susan's house for dinner. When Heather saw me, she began to cry. After watching her mom and I interact, Heather said, "You two are so alike!"

Everyone was so kind and welcoming to Bob and me. We ate and drank and laughed for hours. Jerry was on a nonstop roll with funny jokes and stories. He was absolutely hysterical. It was like we had known each other forever.

The next day we had a lovely lunch on the nearby lake and then we went antique shopping. Susan and I discovered that we both love antique shopping. It's in our blood! After lunch we visited my niece, Heather, at her lovely Victorian home. Before we left, Heather said, "Aunt Susie, you are my favorite aunt." I had only known Heather for about twenty-four hours. Her comment made me feel so special and loved. She was so sweet to say those words to me!

Heather, me, Jerry, Susan, and Chris, 2017

The next morning, we drove to a nearby town to do some site seeing. Bob and I were sitting in the backseat. Bob watched Susan as she gave Jerry directions, using her hands as she spoke. After a few minutes,

Bob said, "Oh my God. You two are so much alike. You have the same mannerisms!"

The next day we drove back to T.K.'s house and spent a couple of days with my sisters and their families before we had to leave. It was so hard to say good-bye. On the way to the airport, we stopped one final time at Susan's for a brief good-bye on the way to the airport. I'll never forget Chris saying to Bob, "Take care of my sister." I just loved hearing those words, from the brother I always wanted. I hugged both Susan and Chris for the longest time. I didn't want to leave my new siblings I had waited so long to meet.

Family

Not long after we returned, I received a card from Susan, which read, "I was always wishing for a sister—but I never imagined having a sister as wonderful as you!!! I am blessed to have you in my life. I know we will have many good times."

And we have! In September 2018, Susan and Jerry came to California for a visit. Jerry was looking at all of my family photos. All of a sudden, he said, "I didn't know that our son Bryan came out here for a visit."

Tracy and Jason in Thailand, 2018

He was looking at a picture of my kids, Tracy and Jason. He thought Jason was their son, Bryan. He couldn't believe how much they looked alike. We all laughed. On the first day of their visit, we surprised them, and invited some friends and family over for a party. I wanted to introduce everyone to meet my new sister and brother-in-law. Of course, everyone loved them. We had such a wonderful time. The next day we went to Malibu for lunch and afterward we walked along the beach.

Susan and Jerry were only able to stay for a few days, and it went by too fast.

Susan and me, 2018

In 2018, Susan and Jerry's daughter, Heather, her husband, Travis, and their son, Edward, also came out for a visit. Tracy and Jeff joined us for a BBQ and we all laughed and talked late into the evening.

The next day we took them to lunch in Malibu and talked and laughed some more. Tracy and Heather are about the same age and bonded immediately. We went back to Tracy's house and ate, drank, and had so much fun.

Me, Tracy, and Heather (Susan's daughter), 2018

Heather's daughter, Skyler, and her boyfriend, Matt, also made a trip out to Los Angeles. They came to our house and then went to Malibu and hung out at the beach with Tracy and Jeff.

A week after my first trip to New York, T.K.'s daughter, Heather, and her husband, Brad, traveled to Thailand, and they were able to meet up with Jason as I had hoped. It meant so much to Jason that they wanted to meet. They chatted for hours, closing down the restaurant. Jason said they made him feel like they had known him their whole lives.

Brad, Jason, and Heather (T.K.'s daughter) in Thailand, 2016

In the summer of 2019, my sister T.K. and her husband, Paul, came for a quick visit. They had flown to Northern California for a seminar in the wine country. Beforehand, T.K. told Paul, "I'm not going unless we can go to Los Angeles to see my sister." Of course, he made it happen.

As soon as T.K. got out of the car, she ran up to the front door to give me a big hug. Tracy and Jeff also came, and we had a lovely dinner outside by the pool. They were only able to stay one night, but having my sister under my roof felt like a dream come true. I'm so blessed that all three of my sisters have now come out to visit us. I'm hoping one day my brother Chris can come for a visit as well.

T.K. and me, 2019

• • •

As I sit here at my dad's desk, in my mom and dad's house that they gifted me, I am reflecting on how truly blessed I am. My dad spent so many hours at this desk, raising money for their synagogue and working to better their community. My dad was truly the synagogue's patriarch, and my mom was the matriarch.

Mom and Dad, 2000

Me and Bob, 2018

Bob and I will celebrate our thirty-fifth anniversary in January 2022. I couldn't have asked for a better husband. He is amazing and spoils me rotten.

I already know how lucky I am to have my beautiful children, their spouses, and my precious granddaughter. I'm also very lucky to have Bob's two adult children, Don and Heidi, whom I consider my own. Don lives in New Mexico. Heidi, her husband, and their children live in Washington State. We see them as often as we can.

Jason; his wife, Nana; and their daughter, Naiya 2020

Heidi and Don, 2018

I think about my parents, Morrie and Rose, and I get very emotional. I am surrounded by so many memories of them and my grandparents. I still have my grandmother's trendle sewing machine, from the year 1910. I have my dad's baby chair and bronzed baby shoes, also from the year 1910. I have the one-hundred-year-old bell that my dad's mom used to ring to call everyone in for dinner, when they were at their cottage on Lake Muskegon in Michigan. I have my grandfather's transistor radio from the early 1970s on which he used to listen to the L.A. Dodgers games while the family was out by the pool. He loved those Dodgers, and that radio. I also have some of my mom's china and crystal from my parents' wedding in 1935. I have so many other lovely mementos of my parents.

Our home has become the party house, as it was when my parents lived here. Five years ago, my cousin Karen and I decided to have a first-time cousins' reunion at our home. We invited all of our cousins, approximately sixty from all over the state and a few from out of state. We wound up with about forty family members. It was so nice to carry on the tradition that my parents started, always having both sides of the family at all of our get-togethers.

Now I have my newfound family, the family I never knew existed before April 2016. I couldn't be more blessed. I thank God every day for my wonderful life.

I couldn't have handpicked three better sisters. They are so amazing and welcomed me without any hesitation. We love each other so much. My brother Chris also welcomed me with open arms. His thoughtfulness and love have been overwhelming. My siblings' love and acceptance mean more than I can explain.

My search involved a lot of time and effort, and it resulted in some real heartbreak, but it was all worth it. I now have the siblings I always wanted, and I have close relationships with their spouses and children. I have received more love from them than I ever could have imagined.

I am eternally grateful to my best friend Linda and my dear friend Jane. Without them, I wouldn't have begun my search again, and I wouldn't have found my family. I thank God every day for the two of them, for unselfishly helping me in my search.

Me and Linda, 2019

Jane, Tracy, and me in Tracy's art gallery, 2018

I am also thankful to Gail, for making this book possible. I never could have done it without her.

If you are searching for your birth parents, you will hit road-blocks, just like I did, but don't give up. There are so many resources out there to help: Ancentry.com, 23 and Me, MyHeritage.com, Classmates. com, Newspapers.com, WhitePages.com, and many more. Where one door shuts, another might open. You have to persevere, even when you feel like quitting. I couldn't have asked for a more beautiful family, but I would have missed out if I had stopped searching. I'm so thankful I kept pushing forward with my search.